SI for Early Intervention
A Team Approach

Edited by Katherine Newton Inamura, M.A., OTR

Photos by Shay McAtee

**Therapy
Skill Builders®** ®
a division of
The Psychological Corporation
555 Academic Court
San Antonio, Texas 78204-2498
1-800-228-0752

Disclaimer

To the best of the editor's knowledge, no instruction or other material in this work is inaccurate or will result in injury to anyone if used properly and in accordance with the directions.

Reproducing Pages From This Book

As described below, some of the pages in this book may be reproduced for instructional use (not for resale). To protect your book, make a photocopy of each reproducible page. Then use that copy as a master for photocopying.

This book is dedicated to Dr. A. Jean Ayres, who was devoted to the pursuit of knowledge about sensory integration and the use of that knowledge to empower children and their families. She continues to inspire us, whether we are theoreticians, researchers, or clinicians.

Introduction

This book has been written to present the Milestones program, which is an example of a sensory integration-based early intervention program. Milestones, which uses a team approach, was originally developed at the Ayres Clinic, but has been the model for programs elsewhere. The Ayres Clinic is a treatment center founded by Dr. A. Jean Ayres, the pioneer of sensory integration theory and treatment techniques. Dr. Ayres was the first to develop the concept that sensory integration influences more complex learning and behavior. She identified sensory integration as the brain's process of organizing and interpreting information from the senses (balance, gravity, position, movement, touch, smell, taste, vision, and hearing). She developed a treatment approach for children with sensory integrative dysfunction that involves the children in activities providing enriched sensory experiences and requiring adaptive responses.

Milestones is an early intervention group program designed to use sensory integration principles to facilitate all areas of a young child's development. In this program, which was offered at the Ayres Clinic until 1996, the children engage in activities designed to challenge their ability to adapt appropriately to incoming sensory information with successful, organized responses. Parents are encouraged to participate with their children so that the program staff and the family can form a more effective team.

The first chapter of this book identifies the importance of sensory integration to the development of infants and toddlers. Chapter two briefly identifies principles of sensory integration treatment and other theoretical frameworks that are influential to the design and implementation of the program. The majority of this chapter delineates the program's design in terms of the participants, routine, and the environment and objects. More than fifty activities of the Milestones program are described in the third chapter. Chapter four discusses the ways in which the staff works as a team and in collaboration with families to manage this program. The fifth chapter provides case examples of children who participated in the program. Finally, there are appendixes that make suggestions concerning forms and resources for materials and equipment.

Acknowledgments

The preliminary preparation of this book for publication was supported administratively and financially by the Ayres Clinic and Sensory Integration International. This book is the result of the collaborative effort of many people over an extended period. As a number of people who contributed to the creation of this book are not listed as authors, I wish to recognize their participation in the process. Additionally, there are a few who deserve special recognition for their extra degree of support. These individuals include:

Erna Imperatore Blanche, Ph.D., OTR

Elise Holloway, M.PH., OTR

Zoe Mailloux, M.A., OTR, FAOTA

Wendolyn Houghton Martin, M.A., CCC-SLP

Victoria McGuire, B.S. Ed.

Milestones Children and Families (1989–1995)

Milestones Staff (1989–1995)

My husband, Ken, and children, Suzanne, Carolyn, and Stuart

Terri Chew Nishimura, M.A., OTR

Lori Shaw, M.Ed.

Patricia S. Webster, M.A., OTR

About the Editor

Katherine Newton Inamura was coordinator of early intervention services at the Ayres Clinic in Torrance, Calif., when she created and directed Milestones, an early intervention, interdisciplinary group program. She studied and trained under the tutelage of Dr. A. Jean Ayres and started at the Ayres Clinic as a work-study program participant during graduate school. Ms. Inamura attained the positions of research assistant, senior therapist, and then clinical associate before accepting the Milestones challenge. She is certified as an occupational therapist by the National Board of Certification in Occupational Therapy Inc. Ms. Inamura also is certified to administer and interpret sensory integration and praxis tests by Sensory Integration International, and is trained to evaluate administrators of these tests. She received a B.S. and an M.A. in Occupational Therapy from the University of Florida and the University of Southern California, respectively. Ms. Inamura has made presentations at conferences and published articles in professional journals such as *Sensory Integration Quarterly* about the Milestones program and sensory integration. She now works as an independent consultant.

Contents

2   Milestones Program Structure: Why, Who, What, Where, and When   45

3   Activities   81

Kayra Emmons, Katherine Newton Inamura, Kirsti
Kela, Elisabeth Knauss, Corinne Koba-Moody, Victoria
McGuire, Terri Chew Nishimura, Patricia S. Webster,
and Nancy Wolfinger

4   Program Management: How to Make it Work   153

Katherine Newton Inamura, Patricia S. Webster,
Zoe Mailloux, Terri Chew Nishimura, and
Victoria McGuire

5   Case Examples: How the Program Worked   171

Patricia S. Webster, Katherine Newton Inamura,
and Victoria McGuire

Tables

CHAPTER 1

The Impact of Sensory Processing on Early Child Development

Erna Imperatore Blanche, Ph.D., OTR

During the past decades, there has been a substantial shift in the conceptualization of infant development. Present theories emphasize the concept of the child's developmental process as influenced by an interplay of many variables including genetic and environmental factors and the relationship between the brain, the body, and the environment (Lockman and Thelen 1993; Short-Degraff 1988; Shumway-Cook and Woollacott 1995). This chapter focuses on the importance of sensory experiences on the infant's overall development. Emphasis will be placed on the impact of sensory processing on motor, cognitive, and social-emotional areas of development, the integration of these processes in praxis, and the performance of daily activities including play. The chapter is divided into two parts. Part 1 summarizes basic principles of development and their application to clinical practice. Part 2 illustrates the impact of sensory processing on different areas of development, and the purposeful outcome of normal development: praxis and organization of daily occupations. Furthermore, this chapter presents examples from current literature to lend support to Dr. A. Jean Ayres' view of development as influenced by sensory integration.

Part 1   General Concepts About Child Development and Their Application to Clinical Practice

Some of the most common concepts in normal development include the interplay between nature and nurture, the view of the child as an active agent in her own development, and the unfolding of increased organizational abilities throughout the first years of life. These concepts have changed in several ways during the past decade.

The Importance of Nature and Nurture (Genes and Environment)

The two most popular frames of reference used to understand child development are the biological-maturation perspective, which identifies biological heritage as the major cause of development, and the environmental-learning perspective, which identifies environmental influence through learning as pivotal in the child's development (Cole and Cole 1989). These frames no longer are considered mutually exclusive; both are used to explain some aspects of development.

The biological or genetic factors are defined as "changes that result from the aging process . . . rather than from learning, injury, or other life experiences" (Shaffer 1988, 31). Genetic factors are determined by heredity, which may play a role in the intellectual development of the individual in three ways: by determining physical structures; by programming automatic behavioral reactions, such as reflexes; and by regulating tendencies to adapt and organize (Piaget 1952; Ginsburg and Opper 1969). Heredity is believed to influence 30% of an individual's beliefs, 30% of some psychiatric disorders, and 40% of specific cognitive abilities and personality (Plomin 1990).

Environmental factors are defined as the experiences occurring in one's life that impact development. These experiences are derived from the participation in specific occupations available to the individual. The environmental influence includes externally generated information from the immediate physical environment (Gottlieb 1983) and the history of the broader social-cultural group to which the child belongs (Bronfenbrenner 1979; Bruner 1986).

In addition, development is influenced by the individual's health (Gilfoyle, Grady, and Moore 1981) and the interaction between different systems in the individual (Lockman and Thelen 1993; Shumway-Cook and Woollacott 1995). Repeated illness or malnutrition are some of the general health factors that may affect the child's development.

Hence, the child's development is shaped by biological factors, interaction with the environment within a specific culture, and the dynamic interaction among processes occurring in the child's different systems as they are exposed to the external environment (Lockman and Thelen 1993; Short-Degraff 1988; Shumway-Cook and Woollacott 1995).

In reference to sensory experiences, maturation of sensory processing capabilities may follow a predetermined and environment-independent path. Ayres (1979) proposed that there is an innate drive to seek experiences that challenge the individual and provide sensory input. According to Ayres' view, the child further develops the ability to integrate sensory input with each successful interaction with the environment. In this way children contribute to their development. But Majnemer, Brownstein, Kadanoff and Shevell (1992) propose that early exposure of premature infants to extra-uterine environmental influences may contribute to these infants' presentation of a different adaptive capacity when compared with the normal newborn. Simply stated, as long as the child is able to process sensory input adequately, and the environment is typical, maturation will follow the predetermined path. However, this developmental path changes according to the child's sensory environment and, therefore, is different in the child who has atypical sensory processing abilities or the child exposed to an atypical sensory environment.

The importance of sensory experiences during the first years of life is evident in research performed in sensory deprived environments. Observations made of children who spent time in orphanages in Romania show that these youngsters present behaviors that have been associated with sensory processing disorders: bumping the head against a surface, rocking, and pinching and biting themselves. The possibility of reversing the effects of the deprivation is directly related to the length of time the child has been exposed to a deprived environment (Cermak 1996; 1997).

Another example includes studies made with school-age children who spent time in a neonatal intensive care unit (NICU) because of very low birth weight. When tested with chosen subtests of the *Sensory Integration and Praxis Test* (Ayres 1989), these children's scores in finger identification and kinesthesia were significantly correlated with the length of stay in the NICU. The author concludes that decreased performance in basic somatosensory tests may be related to the environmental restrictions that occur in a NICU. (DeMaio-Feldman 1994).

The Child as an Active Participant in Development

Closely related to the nature/nurture concept is the notion of the infant as either a passive recipient or active participant in her own development. The view of the infant as an active agent is prevalent in current literature on normal development. The infant responds to objects and people in the environment by producing adaptive responses. The type of responses may depend on genetic characteristics (e.g., body size), previous interactions with the environment, and/or alternatives in the present. For Sameroff (1975, 67), each contact "between organism and environment is a transaction in which each is altered by the other." The child is an active agent whose developmental process is influenced by her unique transactions with the environment. Therefore, the child is involved in creating the environment that will influence her own development (Brazelton 1973; Bronfenbrenner 1979; Shaffer 1988).

Ayres (1984) stressed the role of the child's active participation by describing the importance of sensory input and the adaptive responses in normal development. An adaptive response is defined as "an appropriate action in which the individual responds successfully to some environmental demand" (Ayres 1979, 181). The impact of the environment over children's development occurs through the integration of sensory experiences made available to them. It is through the senses that the child first learns about space, objects, and people. The sensations are organized by the central nervous system (CNS) through the production of an active response to the stimulus (Ayres 1979). This concept of organizing sensory information through an adaptive response is described by Ayres as the most basic principle of child development. The child acquires meaning from the environment and is able to transact with it through this organization of sensory information.

According to the sensory integration frame of reference, normal development requires several things:

1. An environment that provides sensory input that facilitates an adaptive response;
2. Adequate sensory processing; and
3. The capability of producing an adaptive response that may be evidenced in the motor, cognitive, language, or social-emotional areas (Ayres 1972).

Present theories of motor control support Ayres' assumptions by emphasizing the importance of an interplay between perception, cognition, and movement, and the task in the environment in the acquisition of motor skills (Shumway-Cook and Woollacott 1995). Therefore, although nature provides the foundations for development, and the environment provides the stimuli that may or may not facilitate this development, it is the child's ability to process sensory input and the child's active interaction with the environment that assures learning and development.

Differentiation and Organization

An important concept derived from the study of normal development is the view that it is the tendency for behavior to become more versatile, flexible, and differentiated (Gottlieb 1983; Als 1986). The child's interactions with the environment evolve from primarily reflexive and undifferentiated responses to sensory input to more intentional, differentiated, and adaptive interactions. These more adaptive and intentional interactions are a result of an increased ability to self-organize. Self-organization is endorsed by the dynamical action theory, which proposes that individual parts of a system behave collectively and orderly when they come together (Shumway-Cook and Woollacott 1995). Self-organization requires filtering or regulating sensory input and intersensory integration. For example, the increased ability to organize one's self, which occurs in the infant's attentional system (Als 1986; Brazelton 1973), relies on the infant's capacity to regulate sensory input adequately. The organization of the attentional system is pivotal when learning new skills.

Ayres' original model (1972; 1979) of how sensory processing impacts normal development refers to the concept of differentiation. In this description of development, Ayres (1979) hypothesizes that as the child matures, sensory processing becomes more organized, resulting in greater sensory discrimination and sensory integration.

Greater sensory integration makes more complex adaptive responses possible. In turn, these responses promote the organization of the brain. Furthermore, greater organization of the brain facilitates higher levels of sensory integration (Ayres 1989). Integration not only means the summation of sensory input but also the filtering of superfluous sensory input. This filtering is essential to the organization of the attentional system.

Increased organization also is seen in the development of the more complex skills of praxis, language, and social interactions (all of which rely on the foundation of sensory, motor, and cognitive development), and the use of these skills in progressively more complex transactions in social-cultural environments.

In summary, development is guided by several factors, including the genetic makeup, the sensory experiences available in the immediate environment, the culture to which one belongs, a CNS' ability to process and organize sensory information, and the child's capability of producing an adaptive response to the environment.

Importance of Understanding Normal Development

For clinicians working with developmentally delayed children, studying the development of the typical child can provide a guide to assessment, understanding of the development of compensatory skills, and a frame of reference for intervention.

Guide to Assessment

Early identification of deficit areas is essential to avoiding or lessening further development of difficulties. Understanding normal development assists the professional in determining whether the presence of a specific behavior is within the typical range for that age and culture, or if it is a sign of atypical development. If the child exhibits signs of atypical development, a clinician's understanding of normal development provides a frame of reference that assists in the following ways:

1. Determining whether a behavior is delayed (a behavior that generally is seen at younger ages), or if the behavior is atypical (a behavior that is not part of the typical repertoire);
2. Identifying which functions or areas are delayed and how these functions affect overall performance in daily occupations;
3. Establishing how far behind the infant is functioning in comparison to other children of the same age;
4. Identifying if there is a missing developmental milestone and offering possible explanations for this; and
5. Determining if a specific behavior is functional in the child's environment, even when it is atypical or delayed.

Development of Compensatory Skills

Identifying sensory deficits early in life is important because these deficits become more evident when the demands and expectations placed on the child increase with age. In order to cope with the environmental demands, children who have sensory and/or motor deficiencies often develop compensations. These compensations impact the child's overall performance and may interfere with treatment. The development of compensations often is described in reference to children who exhibit movement difficulties (Bly 1983). These movement compensations are strategies used by the developing child to cope with primary movement difficulties that were not identified early in life. The strategies often result in even more abnormal and/or limiting patterns. Compensations often turn into habits that mask original movement problems and make them more difficult to identify and overcome (Bly 1983).

In the case of a child with sensory processing dysfunction, the problem is presumed to have been present early in life but may not have been identified. By the time the child attends school, he often exhibits motor, social-emotional, cognitive, and academic deficits that have evolved from the sensory processing problem. A knowledgeable clinician recognizes that a child's avoidance of certain types of activities may be related to underlying problems in sensory processing or motor planning. The child may compensate for the sensory processing problem by avoiding challenging situations. For example, children who exhibit tactile modulation deficits may avoid activities that provide touch and thus increase the magnitude of the problem by depriving themselves of the everyday experience of touch. Children who exhibit practic deficits often avoid playing with constructional toys, thus making the problem more severe by self-deprivation of the experience they need to practice most (see Table 1-1 on p. 7).

In summary, studying typical sequences of development assists professionals and parents in refining their observational skills to be able to identify signs of dysfunction during the first years of life, before compensations are well-established and unfavorable consequences result. Understanding qualitative and quantitative differences among children with and without a dysfunction provides a frame of reference that helps professionals differentiate between these populations.

Frame of Reference for Intervention

In addition to guiding assessment, knowledge of child development guides professionals and parents to successful intervention. Studying the different concepts that are to be taken into consideration in normal development provides the professional with an understanding of the impact of these aspects on the child's functional problems. A child who exhibits a sensory processing deficit needs to be assessed and treated for the possible biological and/or environmental base of the problem. The child's avoidance of, or refusal to engage in, situations that augment the impact of the

Table 1-1.   The long-term effects of sensory processing deficits*

ORIGINAL PROBLEMS	COMPENSATIONS	CONSEQUENCES
Sensory Processing Deficit	**Coping Strategy**	**Long-Term Deficits**
Tactile modulation deficits	Avoidance of social situations that require tactile contact	Social isolation
Poor modulation of tactile and/or proprioceptive input	Seeking large amounts of proprioceptive input such as that received when pushing, pinching, hitting, throwing, etc.	Labeled aggressive Behavior problems Acting out
Vestibular processing deficits—inadequate postural control	Leaning on hands Sluggish posture	Rounded upper back
Gravitational insecurity	Staying close to the ground Dragging feet Staying close to supports	Apprehension Insecurity Avoidance of challenging situations
Insecurity	Avoidance of challenging situations	
Poor constructional skills	Avoidance of manipulative play Avoidance of constructional toys	Low frustration tolerance when presented with activities that require two- and three-dimensional copying
Poor motor planning skills	Avoidance of activities that require motor coordination, such as sports	Inadequate physical fitness Overweight Feelings of inadequacy (boys more than girls)

Reprinted with permission. (Blanche 1996)

dysfunction also needs to be considered. In addition, therapists who understand functional performance during development and how these functional skills occur in everyday life can recreate these situations during treatment. Intervention may address a child's missing milestones and their impact on functional performance. However, missing milestones are addressed only if their absence impacts functional performance. In summary, increasing the understanding of normal development refines the focus and efficiency of evaluation and treatment.

Part 2

Praxis and the Organization of Daily Occupations

The ability to become more organized, which is developed during the first few years of life, is evidenced in the development of praxis and performance of daily occupations. Praxis is defined as an aptitude that underlies conceptualization, motor planning, and execution of skilled adaptive interaction with the physical world (Ayres 1985, 1989). Praxis can be further described as the organization of actions in space and time that allows transactions with the environment and is associated with the production of purposeful activity. Praxis does not appear abruptly from one moment to the next; it develops and expands qualitatively as forms of organization differ from one age to the next (Miller 1986).

Praxis also is related to the purposeful performance of occupations. Occupations are defined as " 'chunks' of activity within the ongoing stream of human behavior which are named in the lexicon of the culture" (Yerxa et al. 1990, 5). Organization of chunks of activity into occupations depends on the ability to conceptualize, motor plan, and execute. As organizational skills and praxis increase, so does the ability to organize acts into occupations and occupations into a meaningful daily routine. The ability to create this routine requires sequencing, timing (MacKay 1985), and shaping one's actions in space—processes that are fundamental in praxis (Blanche, unpublished paper). Therefore, praxis is viewed as an organizational process that is evidenced early in motor control; however, as the child grows, praxis is evidenced in organizational skills that encompass larger spatiotemporal worlds (Blanche, unpublished paper).

Development of Praxis

Praxis has been compared to language, in that language is the organization of words into sentences, which in turn are organized into coherent thoughts. Praxis is the organization of components of movements into acts, which in turn are organized into occupations and meaningful daily routines. Language allows transactions in the social world; praxis allows transactions in the physical world. The development of praxis and language are influenced by sensory, motor, and cognitive development. Praxis and language appear when movements no longer are generalized but become purposefully and cognitively controlled.

Influences on the Development of Praxis

Motor control, including postural control and movements in space, is described as the interaction of perception, cognition, and action. Motor control is influenced by the environment and the task at hand (Shumway-

Cook and Woollacott 1995). Praxis, as an organizational skill, requires motor control and, hence, is influenced by these variables.

The perceptual and sensory processing skill that impacts praxis is body scheme, or the perception of one's body, which is essential to one's relationship with the outside world (Ayres 1972, 1979, 1985; Miller 1986). This perception of the body is developed from the sensory and movement experiences early in life (Ayres 1979; Miller 1986). Sensory integration theory (Ayres 1972, 1985; Fisher 1991) links praxis primarily to somatosensory and vestibular processing and the establishment of body scheme. Miller (1986) describes praxis as appearing when the infant develops perception of the body as separate from the external space. Therefore, praxis develops after the infant is able to modulate sensory input from his body and the environment.

The cognitive aspects associated with praxis and motor control are perception, ideation or conceptualization, motor planning, and motivation to activate the action (Ayres 1985; Shumway-Cook and Woollacott 1995). These cognitive components include the ability to develop a goal for one's actions (also referred to as ideation) or conceptualization of the action (Ayres 1985), have a mental representation of the object and the action, and be motivated to initiate the performance. The action components of praxis and motor control include the ability to program an action, initiate the action, organize the movements into a coherent unit that fits the demands of the task and, finally, activate the necessary muscles to execute the action.

Praxis deficits can be differentiated along the parameters of cognition, movement production, and sensation. The sensory processing deficits associated with dyspraxia are described as feedback deficits that may have a tactile or vestibulo-proprioceptive base and feedforward deficits, or a deficit in anticipatory control mechanisms associated with the processing of vestibulo-proprioceptive input (Ayres 1985, 1989; Fisher 1991).

Signs of dyspraxia also can be identified along movement parameters in that inadequate motor planning skills may be evidenced in fine motor or gross motor skills. Examples of deficits in praxis that are apparent in gross motor development include difficulties with climbing, riding a tricycle, or maneuvering obstacles in space. Children diagnosed as having praxis deficits also may exhibit difficulties with fine motor activities such as coloring, handling a spoon, or manipulating small toys. Often one may see children who exhibit difficulties in one area more than another.

Signs of dyspraxia that may suggest a cognitive base are lack of motivation, poor ideation, or decreased cognitive abilities. However, disorders in motor planning or ideation often can be the product of a sensory processing deficit rather than a cognitive dysfunction because cortical areas responsible for ideation and motor planning depend on adequate processing of sensory input, in order to function optimally.

The development of praxis requires basic skills, including the following:

1. *Acquisition of adequate sensory processing skills, which influence the development of a map of one's body, affect the interactions with the physical world, and are pivotal in obtaining information from the*

environment. The creation of these body maps precedes the development of motor planning and ideation during the first year. These maps require adequate processing of vestibular, proprioceptive, and tactile input and are used to compare a desired action with the actual performance of an action. The ability to use sensory information for feedback appears earlier than the ability to use feedforward successfully to program future actions such as balancing and reaching (Shumway-Cook and Woollacott 1995). In addition, praxis requires adequate visual perception skill because the ability to modify one's actions often is dependent upon visual input.

2. *Development of basic action components that can be organized into more complex units of purposeful behavior in order to meet the demands of a novel task and environment.* The child's increasing motor control over his actions influences the development of praxis.

3. *Emergence of cognitive skills: motivation, intention, anticipation, cause and effect, object relations, and basic ideational skills that appear during the first year of life.* This leads to the development of orchestrated patterns of organized behavior or strings of activities into meaningful occupations such as climbing up to the sink to get water.

Developmental Progression of Praxis

Praxis develops in conjunction with sensory, motor, and cognitive skills. Motor planning, an important component of praxis, is evidenced in imitation, copying, and using tools (Ayres 1989). Imitation may be observed even in newborns. The newborn's most impressive ability is to imitate facial expressions (Field 1990). Although this appears to be an automatic behavior that is not well understood, it may suggest that the ability to imitate and copy others is essential in human development. During the first few months, the infant is able to imitate elementary vocal, visual, and grasping movements. At first, the imitation includes only familiar actions (Ginsburg and Opper 1969). However, because praxis is described as the ability to perform unfamiliar tasks, imitation that occurs at this level would not be considered part of this skill.

The development of praxis also can be observed in the development of organizational skills, from mastering the immediate surroundings to mastering the broader environment. At first, infants depend on the adult to satisfy their basic needs, change their position, and provide sensory input. During the next months, they develop basic movement components that enable them to change positions and interact with the immediate space. As the toddler learns to control motor skills, spatial territory is expanded to include a larger external world. The toddler also learns to control a larger temporal world when performing multiple-step activities.

Contributions to the foundation of praxis that occur during the first six months of development can be summarized as follows:

1. Development of body scheme through body exploration and simple movements in space;
2. Increased control over head and trunk musculature;

3. Appearance of intention and immediate anticipation of an action; and
4. Basic imitation skills.

However, we cannot talk of praxis at this age, because object concepts, the understanding of cause and effect, and perception of the body in space have not been fully developed.

During the second six months of life, the infant refines sensory discrimination, movement skills, and cognitive skills. As the infant refines such cognitive skills as intention, imitation, and control over movement in space, these skills influence each other and impact the development of practic skills. During the last few months of the first year of life, the infant develops the ability to imitate unfamiliar actions at approximately the same time she learns to use tools, such as a spoon. The development of body scheme as separate from space, a developmental stage of praxis (Miller 1986), is refined as the child moves through space.

During the second six months of life, the foundation of practic skills is further enhanced by the appearance of:

1. Refinement of sensory discrimination abilities and body scheme;
2. Consistent evidence of intentional and purposeful activity, in that a goal is present from the onset of the action (e.g., placing a cube into a container);
3. The ability to link cause with effect;
4. Object permanence, or maintaining a visual representation of an object or person (precursor to ideation);
5. The ability to relate one object to another (placing cube in cup) as a precursor to constructional praxis;
6. Mobility in space by means of rolling, crawling and, later, walking, all of which facilitate the development of space perception;
7. The ability to accommodate by interrupting and correcting an action, which first appears in the ability to reach and grasp; and
8. The ability to imitate, as evidenced in whole body and oral motor areas.

During the second year, the child spends most of the time mastering and exploring objects (White 1975). Mastering the external world requires and facilitates the development of praxis. The second year of life is pivotal in this development, which depends on sensory processing, motor, and cognitive skills. Because many of the milestones occurring between twelve and twenty-four months of age require basic organizational skills and praxis, evidence of praxis deficits can be seen at this age. The toddler's world expands as she learns to master a larger space; for example, walking from room to room around the house and even venturing to climb low equipment in the park. The toddler moves through space, which offers new experiences. The child then needs to produce alternate plans to attain a goal. Newly attained skills are based on previously developed sensory, motor, and cognitive skills, and increase the repertoire of possible interactions. Additionally, during the second year, toddlers refine the use of tools such as using utensils, crayons, and toys. They also develop basic three-dimensional constructional praxis while building with blocks, and they develop basic two-dimensional graphomotor skills while copying lines.

Ideational skills are observed in the child's imaginary play. Pretend-play starts appearing during the second year of life, as the child substitutes a realistic replica for a real object; for example, pretending to drink from a doll-size cup (Fenson 1985). Pretend-play requires ideation or conceptualization of an object and an action based on a sensory experience. The underlying ideational skills are influenced by the development of symbolic representation and the ability to solve problems in new and creative ways.

Organizational skills also undergo major transformations during the second year of life. The toddler initiates complex activities that require organization of behavior while exploring and interacting with the home environment (Greenspan and Greenspan 1985). Behavior patterns become purposeful and complex and tend to have a beginning, middle, and end (Ayres 1979; Greenspan and Greenspan 1985).

Increased organization of behavior can be observed during play as well. At first, the toddler approaches objects, interacts with them, and shifts attention rapidly to a new activity. These generally are one-step activities. It appears as if the child is "'controlled by' rather than 'in control of' the objects or activities in the immediate environment" (Fenson 1985, 35). During the last semester of the second year, the child starts combining actions into coordinated behavior sequences or multiple-step activities. Fenson provides two examples of organized behavior. One is the child using a spoon to stir a cup and then to stir a pot. This action indicates that the skill of stirring was transferred to different objects. The other example is placing the doll on the bed and then covering it. This indicates the ability to perform sequences of behaviors. The organization of multiple-step behavior expands during the third year.

The practic skills that are developed during the second year include:

1. Ideational skills;
2. Basic organization of behavior;
3. Ability to copy and imitate simple actions; and
4. Enhanced timing of gross motor skills.

In summary, praxis is a product of adequate functioning in many areas of development, and impacts performance in those same areas. For example, cognition impacts adequate development of praxis, and practic problems impacted by sensory processing deficits may impact performance in cognitive tasks. Hence, it is important to identify the specific area that is hindering the development of praxis.

The Components of Purposeful Performance and Praxis

This section describes the influence of the motor, cognitive, social-emotional, and sensory systems on the development of praxis and purposeful occupational performance.

Social-Emotional Development

Cognitive attention and emotional engagement with another human being during an interaction may play a pivotal role in the evolution of the species and the development of the child (Als 1986). Modern theories of social-emotional development are rooted in the importance of self-regulation and emotion regulation. Self-regulation in social-emotional development is described as the ability to monitor one's behavior or the "ability to comply with a request, to initiate and cease activities according to situational demands, to modulate the intensity, frequency, and duration of verbal and motor actions in social-educational settings, to postpone acting upon a desired object or goal, and to generate socially approved behavior in the absence of external monitors" (Kopp 1982, 199–200). Emotion regulation is defined as "an ongoing process of the individual's emotion pattern in relation to moment-by-moment contextual demands" (Cole, Michel, and Teti 1994, 74). Self-regulation is an important aspect in the socialization of children and requires the filtering of incoming sensory input. Kopp (1982) describes five phases of self-regulation that illustrate the importance of sensory motor processes: neurophysiological, sensory motor, control, self-control and self-regulation. These phases begin developing at birth. They are summarized in Table 1-2 on p. 14 and will be described later in this chapter.

Emotions serve the function of coordinating the organism's needs with environmental demands. For example, anger serves the purpose of progressing towards specific goals in the face of obstacles, while sadness serves the purpose of helping the person relinquish a goal and prevent wasted effort. Emotions can have a regulatory influence on other processes and, in turn, need to be regulated to meet the demands of a situation (Cole, Michel, and Teti 1994).

The process of acquiring emotional regulation depends on internal and external factors. These factors contribute to the individual differences in regulation that can be observed among children. Calkins (1994) identifies five sources of emotion regulation—three internal and two external to the child.

The internal sources are the neuroregulatory systems, the behavioral traits, and the cognitive components. The neuroregulatory sources include physiological aspects such as heart rate, brain electrical activity, and endocrine response. The behavioral traits represent and interplay with biological reactivity and thus imply sensory reactivity to particular events. Behavioral traits include attentiveness, interest level, adaptability/reactivity to novelty, and soothability. Cognitive components include social referencing, beliefs, and expectations.

Table 1-2. Self-regulation, self-organization, social-emotional development, and sensory processing*

Author	Transitions in Control Over Self and Environment			
Als, Lester, and Brazelton 1979; Als 1986	Control over autonomic system	Control over motor system	Organization over state organizational system, and Control over cognitive and affective world	
Kopp 1982	Neurophysiological modulation	Sensory motor regulation	Control and self-control—awareness of the demands in the social and physical environment—ability to initiate, maintain, and end an activity	Self-regulation—flexibility over control process—change according to situation
Greenspan and Greenspan 1985	Regulated state while reaching to the external environment	Increased interest in the human world	Discrimination of caretaker—Dialogue with adult (cause and effect in the social world)	Organization of units into patterns and self-control
Sensory Integration Theory	Modulation—internal states	Modulation of sensory input in the environment Experiences of pleasure, anger, excitement, distress, and surprise are elicited by sensory input	Discrimination of sensory input—also requires that timing of response be in synch with incoming input Cognitive prerequisite: intention, goal-direction, awareness of self and action (Kopp 1982)	Discrimination and organization of perceptual experiences Praxis, strategy production, and organization of behavior

Based on Als, Lester, and Brazelton 1979; Als 1986; Greenspan and Greenspan 1985; Kopp 1982.

The external sources are the interactive caregiving styles and the explicit training given to the child in later years. These sources play a pivotal role in the development of self-regulation and can contribute significantly to later performance. Caregiving styles include level of responsiveness and level of cooperation, accessibility, acceptance, and type of support provided. The caregiver's style of interaction and the child's internal sources are combined to produce variations in the emotion regulation.

Greenspan and Greenspan (1985) describe several phases of emotional milestones in the development of the child from birth to four years of age. These overlap with each other and can be viewed as the application of cognitive processes to feelings and social interactions. Table 1-2 summarizes these phases and relates them to sensory processing.

Atypical Development

In literature describing sensory processing, self-regulation is related to modulation of sensory input. Children who have difficulty regulating sensory input may appear irritable and difficult to calm.

Inadequate self-regulation also is described as a marker of a developmental disorder. For example, children with Fragile-X often exhibit signs of poor self-regulation: self-injurious behaviors, excessive tantrums, and repetitive motor behaviors. Children with drug and alcohol exposure exhibit sleep problems, irritability, hyperexcitability, and/or lethargy. Children in the autism spectrum exhibit self-stimulation, sensory sensitivities, and hyperactivity. Children with Rett syndrome exhibit teeth-grinding and facial tics after the first six months of development (Neisworth, Bagnato, and Salvia 1995). These behaviors can be related to difficulties in the processing of sensory input.

Development of Sensory Processing Skills

Sensory processing is defined as the ability to register sensory input, derive information about the stimulus, and store information about the stimulus so that it can be used as a basis for perception and action in the future (Busey and Loftus 1994). Based on Kopp (1982), one can infer that deriving information from a stimulus in the external environment requires the ability to use neurophysiological mechanisms to self-regulate internal states and sensory motor mechanisms to self-regulate in the presence of a variety of external sensory events. Simply stated, the infant needs to be able to regulate the internal state of his body before he can become interested in the external environment (see Table 1-2). For example, a child whose body temperature fluctuates and who cannot reach a level of homeostasis will exhibit decreased interest in exploring the environment.

Research on an infant's development of sensory processing skills has many discrepancies, including the reported age at which a specific skill is observed. According to Haith (1993), these discrepancies are due to the research strategies used to study the presence of perceptual skills. Some researchers emphasize the appearance of components of perceptual skills at earlier ages while others focus on the functional use of that specific skill at a later age.

According to Field (1990, 27), the order of sensory development (touch, vestibular, taste, smell, hearing, and vision) "is the same order in which the sensory areas of the brain develop, and the order in which the world is experienced, first in the womb (where sensory experiences encompass all but the visual sense) and then in the outside world." The sensory systems also follow a proximal-to-distal sequence as the tactile, vestibular, proprioceptive, gustatory (taste), and olfactory (smell) senses that provide information about the body, its position in space and input that is in close proximity develop before the vision and hearing senses that provide information about the external world that is not in direct contact with the body. The influence of tactile, proprioceptive, and vestibular input over an infant's responses decreases early in life as the visual and auditory systems take a more dominant role in interacting with the environment. Although the visual system becomes dominant after the first few months of life, the tactile, vestibular, and proprioceptive systems develop early and therefore greatly influence the child's present and future transactions with the environment (Ayres 1972, 1979).

Sensory input can have three dimensions that together produce a specific sensation or sensory experience. The dimensions are qualitative—the identification of the nature of the stimulus; quantitative—the perception of the intensity of the stimulus; and affective—the amount of pleasure or displeasure connected to the experience (Young 1959 in Cabanac 1988). Most sensory experiences elicit indifferent sensations. The affective quality attached to a sensory input is related to the nature and intensity of the stimuli (Cabanac 1988). Primary positive stimuli are probably chemical (i.e., taste), thermal (i.e., warmth), or mechanical (i.e., touch). One may add that the affective quality of a stimulus also is related to the person's reactivity to the input. For example, children who have a low threshold for tactile input or do not have the regulatory mechanisms to modulate the input may experience a neutral sensation of touch as being intense and therefore unpleasant.

Motor Development

Theories of motor control have undergone significant changes during the past ten years. Motor development, described in the past as proceeding cephalocaudally (head to toe) and proximal-to-distal (Connor et al. 1978; Gilfoyle, Grady, and Moore 1981), is now viewed as being impacted by increased self-organization occurring in a dynamic interaction between the individual's mechanical, psycho-social, and perceptual subsystems (Heriza 1991; Lockman and Thelen 1993; Shumway-Cook and Woollacott 1995). In this new paradigm of motor development, practice and repetition are important in acquiring increased flexibility and adaptability during the developmental process.

Shumway-Cook and Woollacott (1995), among others, proposed that motor control is achieved through a synthesis of perception, action, and cognition in relation to the individual's interaction with a task in the environment. Action requires biomechanical as well as neuromuscular skills that are evidenced in the ability to stabilize the body via postural control and the ability to move the body through space. Postural control is defined as the regulation of "the body's position in space for the dual purposes of stability and orientation" and requires the ability to process sensory information (Shumway-Cook and Woollacott 1995, 459).

Table 1-3.   The tactile system—development and integration*
of input

SENSORY SYSTEM	MODULATION/ REGULATION	DISCRIMINATION	END PRODUCTS
	Arousal Level	Localization	
TACTILE SYSTEM R E G I S T R A T I O N	Mother/infant bond Oral comfort Emotional comfort	Feeding Stereognosis Body percept/ scheme Hand manipulation skills Oral motor skills	Self-esteem Praxis Ability to concentrate

*Reprinted with permission. (Blanche 1996)

Table 1-4.   The proprioceptive system—development and integration of input*

SENSORY SYSTEM	MODULATION/ REGULATION	DISCRIMINATION	END PRODUCTS
	Arousal Level/Protection	Localization	
PROPRIOCEPTIVE SYSTEM	*internal → external* Gravitational security Comfort with changes in position Comfort in weight-bearing patterns (proximal joint stability)	Calibrating spatial and temporal frames of reference Body percept/maps Grading the force of contraction Timing of movement Perception of movement Movement feedback (internalization of movement patterns) Muscle tone Righting reactions Equilibrium reactions Postural control	Coordinated movement Praxis—feedforward Stereognosis

*Reprinted with permission. (Blanche 1995)

Table 1-5.   The vestibular system—development and integration of input**

SENSORY SYSTEM		MODULATION/ REGULATION	DISCRIMINATION	END PRODUCTS
		Arousal Level Protection	Localization	
	registration of input	Bond with gravity	Equilibrium reactions	Praxis—feedforward
		Enjoyment when moved in space	Postural control	Oculomotor control during movement
			Muscle tone	
VESTIBULAR SYSTEM				Language
			Oculomotor control	
			Bilateral motor coordination	
			Timing/sequencing	

**Reprinted with permission. (Blanche 1996)*

   Motor control includes fine motor skills, which are evidenced in visually directed reach and grasp, bimanual control, and hand manipulation. In turn, the development of fine motor control influences other aspects of development, such as intrinsic motivation or mastery motivation. Karniol (1989) proposed that manual manipulation plays a role in the acquisition of perceived control, in that the infant, through interaction with objects, learns about the object's limitations and capabilities and about his own abilities and limitations. Therefore, decreased mastery over objects impacts the child's perceived sense of efficacy.

   Motor development is influenced by and, in turn, influences sensory processing. Reflexes are sensory based. Postural control requires processing vestibular, visual, and somatosensory information. Reach and grasp rely on visual, tactile, and proprioceptive input. Motor development influences the regulation of sensory input in that youngsters who develop basic sensory motor skills use them to regulate sensory information.

Development of Cognitive Skills and Learning

A child acquires most of the cognitive and learning skills necessary for later performance during the first two years of life (Field 1990). The learning of new behaviors can be explained from the brain-maturation, environmental, and interactive perspectives (Cole and Cole 1989). Regardless of the theory used to explain cognitive development and learning, sensory processing plays a crucial role.

   The maturation perspective views development and learning of new behaviors as the result of increased interconnections occurring in the brain independently of environmental input (Cole and Cole 1989). Research on animals that focuses on the effect of enriched and deprived environments suggests that this is an unlikely explanation. This research points to the

Table 1-6. The sensory systems—development and integration of input*

SENSORY SYSTEM	MODULATION/REGULATION	DISCRIMINATION	END PRODUCTS
	Arousal Level		
VISCERAL	*internal → external homeostasis* Rhythms		
GUSTATORY/ OLFACTORY SYSTEM		Feeding	
TACTILE SYSTEM	**Emotional comfort** Mother/infant bond Oral comfort **Emotional comfort**	Stereognosis Body percept/scheme Hand manipulation skills Oral motor skills	Self-esteem
PROPRIOCEPTIVE SYSTEM	**Emotional comfort** Gravitational security Comfort with changes in position	Calibrating spatial and temporal frames of reference Body percept/maps Grading the force of contraction Timing of movement	Praxis (feedback) Ability to concentrate Perception of space Perception of time
VESTIBULAR SYSTEM	Comfort in weight-bearing patterns (proximal joint stability) **Emotional comfort** Gravitational security Enjoyment when moved in space	Perception of movement Movement feedback (internalization of movement patterns) Muscle tone Postural control Bilateral motor integration	Organization of behavior into meaningful activities Praxis— feedforward
VISUAL SYSTEM		Oculomotor control Visual perception (space, depth, etc.)	Visual skills during movement
AUDITORY SYSTEM			Language

Vertical column headings in MODULATION/REGULATION: REGISTRATION, HABITUATION (repeated)

Vertical column headings at right: LEISURE, PLAY, WORK; ACTIVITIES OF DAILY LIVING

Reprinted with permission. (Blanche 1995)

importance of the environment in the development of the brain and subsequent adaptive skills (Diamond et al. 1985).

An example of the environmental perspective is the behaviorist theory, which proposes that development occurs as a consequence to learning. Learning is defined as "relatively permanent change in behavior brought about by the experience of events in the environment" (Cole and Cole 1989). Learning occurs through habituation, operant conditioning, classical conditioning, and contingent social stimulation. Habituation is the weakening of a response to environmental stimuli. The infant who stops responding to specific types of sensory stimuli shows evidence of habituation. Operant conditioning is the modification of an existing response while establishing a relationship with a reinforcer. For example, infants learn to tip the bottle to obtain milk. Classical conditioning is learning to pair an existing response to a new stimulus, such as when a child learns that crying, which has been used until now to express distress, can be used to obtain the mother's attention. Contingent social stimulation occurs when social input, such as the mother's talking, is used to increase the infants' social interactions (Field 1990). In learning new skills, the infant needs to discriminate and filter the environmental input and respond to it successfully.

According to Piaget's interactionist perspective on cognition, developmental reflexes provide a basis for learning new behavior. Through assimilation and accommodation, initial actions are transformed into new actions. Assimilation is the process through which the child takes in new information and transforms it to fit an existing pattern of activity. Accommodation is the process through which the child tries to fit her existing actions to the environment (Ginsburg and Opper 1969; Cole and Cole 1989).

An important psychological force in the development of a child's cognitive and motor skills is the development of mastery motivation or intrinsic motivation and self-concept. Mastery motivation can be defined as the "impetus to achieve and improve one's skills in the absence of any physical reward" (Busch-Rossnagel 1997, 1). It develops during the first years of life and contributes to a child's sense of being an active successful agent in the environment as well as to his self-concept. Mastery motivation has an affective expression and an object-oriented expression. The affective expression is described as pride, and the object-oriented expression is referred to as autonomy (Busch-Rossnagel 1997).

Self-concept, which is related to mastery motivation, also is developed during the first years of life and relates to self-regulation as well as perceptual development. DesRosiers and Busch-Rossnagel (1997) identify six phases in the development of self-concept: self-recognition, a perceptual process; self-representation, a cognitive process; self-description, a language-mediated process; self-assertion, a motivational process; self-evaluation, an emotional process; and self-regulation, a social process.

It is important to be aware that the most basic skills in intellectual and social development are related to the ability to be alert for a time and orient oneself toward the source of the incoming information. These skills are present in the newborn child (Brazelton 1973). Maintaining an alert state requires the ability to filter sensory input so that a state of self-organization or self-regulation can be reached (see Figure 1-1 on p. 21).

In reference to the development of language, Ayres (1985) believes that praxis and language are closely related. This association can be observed

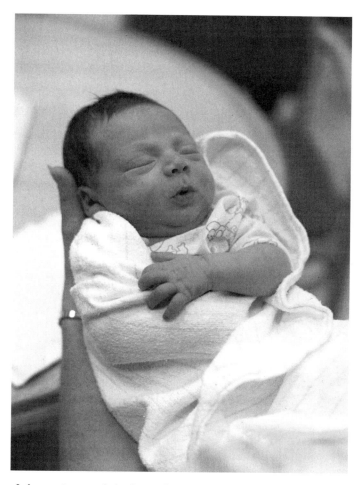

Figure 1-1. **Adequate modulation of sensory information from his body and the environment allows this newborn infant to regulate his state of arousal.** Photo by Shay McAtee.

during normal development in the child's organization of actions into strings of events and the parallel organization of words into sentences. Children who exhibit sensory processing disorders often also exhibit oral motor problems and, later, speech and language disorders.

Language is closely related to auditory processing and cognitive and social-emotional development (White 1975). Speech as a part of oral communication is related to oral sensory motor abilities. During the first two years of life, before language emerges (Field 1990, 1), the infant communicates emotions through facial expressions and sounds that lay the foundation for the use of verbal language. At first, children communicate primarily through crying. They make simple vocalizations but are not interested in listening to the vocalization of others (White 1975). Later, during the first six months of life, infants learn to vocalize in response to an adult's voice. The children make mostly vowel sounds and start to express displeasure by making sounds rather than crying. Early vocalizations serve the purpose of initiating and prolonging interactions with the caregiver, and they impact social interactions.

Developmental Trends During the First Three Years of Life
Birth to Six Months

From birth on, children are challenged to organize sensory input (Greenspan and Greenspan 1985) into adaptive responses. This requires self-regulation. The full-term newborn comes into the world with the ability to self-regulate through neurophysiological mechanisms. Once the infant is in contact with the external environment, self-organization and self-regulation are manifested by the integration of sensory motor mechanisms, such as the smooth transition between the sleep, alert, awake, and aroused states, without taxing physiologic regulation (Als, Lester, and Brazelton 1979, 177).

The integration of motoric and physiological regulation into state control is mastered through adaptation to and interaction with sensory input provided by the caregiver. When these capacities are mastered, the baby then is able to interact with objects and people without taxing basic systems (Als et al. 1979). This phase of self-regulation is called sensory motor self-modulation (Kopp 1982).

The emotional responses present early in life are pleasure, excitement, distress, surprise, and anger (Greenspan and Greenspan 1985). These responses are elicited by environmental and social interaction through the senses. For instance, pleasure is present when the child is held, rocked, and fed. Distress may be triggered by rapidly lowering the infant in space and eliciting a Moro reflex. Anger may be elicited by delayed feeding. Fear and sadness are added to the original repertoire at eight to nine months (Greenspan and Greenspan 1985).

After birth, the infant becomes increasingly more aware and responsive to external social interactions rather than inner physical sensations (Greenspan and Greenspan 1985). Als (1986) provided a glimpse of how the response to external events contributes to transactions between the newborn and adult. For example, the infant may momentarily regard the adult's eyes or show a gesture that appears to be a smile (Morris, 1991). The adult responds to these first momentary reflexive smiles with vocalizations and animated facial expressions which, in turn, increase the baby's arousal and help stabilize her periods of alertness. In this way, the adult and child modify each other's behaviors. The reflexive smile is replaced by a general smile in response to any human face, at about four weeks of age; and, at about five to six months of age, by a more specific smile directed to people who have close contact with the baby (Morris, 1991). Interacting with the adult corresponds to the third milestone described by Greenspan and Greenspan (1985). It occurs between three and ten months of age and is the application of cause and effect to the social world.

The preference for attending to human faces and voices is considered an inherited human behavior (White 1975; Field 1990). Until he is five to six months old, the infant may not show specific attachment to the primary caretaker. Discrimination between the primary caretaker and strangers at this age may occur on the basis of smell, touch, and handling style (proprioceptive feedback) (Connor et al. 1978). This may be another way in which sensory discrimination plays a role in the emotional attachment between the child and caregiver.

In relation to the development of sensory motor control, the newborn's posture is asymmetrical and primarily influenced by flexor muscle tone (Als 1986; Bly 1983). At this time (birth to six months), the infant develops the ability to raise himself against gravity and differentiate movement. Antigravity extensor-motor control develops before antigravity flexor-motor control. It is first evidenced when the baby is placed in a prone position and he attempts to raise his head and later his trunk from the supporting surface. Flexion against gravity is demonstrated in the supine position when the baby lifts her head, upper trunk, lower trunk, and pelvis off of the surface to attempt to roll, or when she brings her hands to her knees and feet. As the child matures, flexor and extensor muscles work in conjunction to gain control over lateral movements and rotation. Trunk rotation is first used in rolling and later in sitting and standing (Bly 1983).

In reference to sensory processing, at birth the tactile, vestibular, olfactory, and proprioceptive systems are mature. The importance of touch in the social-emotional interaction between the child and adult cannot be overemphasized. Early on, the infant is held, caressed, and touched often during the daily routine (see Figure 1-1 on p. 21). Through touch, the baby derives pleasure and establishes the first emotional contact with the caregiver (Montagu 1978; Field 1990). The child soon establishes contact by actively interacting, including moving the hand towards the face of the adult, and integrating tactile, proprioceptive, and visual information with social gratification.

The newborn also exhibits adaptive motor responses linked to localization and discrimination of tactile input. Examples include the grasp reflex in response to touch and discriminating between the nipple and the skin around it during feeding (Colangelo, Bergen, and Gottlieb 1976; Farber 1982).

Integration of tactile and proprioceptive input is important in the development of righting reactions, weight bearing/shifting patterns, hand functions, and oral motor control, starting at birth. For instance, asymmetric tactile and proprioceptive input elicits lateral righting reactions; tactile and proprioceptive input are necessary for the development of hand functions for weight bearing and manipulation. Weight bearing and weight shifting on the palms of the hands evolve from placing the weight on fisted hands to placing it on open hands (Exner 1989). The baby adjusts the position of the hand in response to the information received from the supporting surface. In addition, tactile and proprioceptive input later plays a role in grasp. Processing sensory information from the hand is important to skillfully contouring the hand around a held object and developing fine motor skills. Some of the newborn's actions that are elicited by proprioceptive input include traction responses in the upper extremities (Exner 1989), neck righting reactions, and the asymmetric tonic neck reflex (Fiorentino 1963; Bly 1983).

The vestibular sense is fully developed at birth. Vestibular information is integrated with proprioceptive information and visual information to guide the child's motor actions against gravity. The development of these skills allows the child to raise the head off the supporting surface and extend against gravity.

The olfactory and gustatory senses also develop early in life. Both senses appear to be functional at birth and even in utero. Although olfactory impairments in adults produce alterations in taste and may result in the individual exposing himself to environments with dangerous odors, there is little systematic research on the importance of olfaction during the first months of life (Graziadei 1990). The importance may lie in its influence on the development of the mother-child bond (Greenspan and Greenspan 1985). Sensory deprivation or inadequate processing of this input may impact this interaction.

Mistretta (1990) summarizes the literature on the development of taste and reports that taste buds are among the first sensory receptors to appear in utero, and that newborns and premature infants have a functional sense of taste in that they are able to discriminate between different sensations. The amniotic fluid provides a rich environment composed of water, salts, sugars, and other chemicals and in which the fetus has ample opportunity to experience the sensation of taste. Early in life, there appears to be a preference for sugars, an aversion to acid and bitter tastes, and no discrimination of salt. After birth, taste buds continue to increase in number and morphology (shape). This increase as well as the increased experiences with food may contribute to the significant developmental changes in food preferences and aversions in taste throughout life.

The newborn's visual skills have been studied extensively in recent years and found to be much more sophisticated than previously believed. For example, newborns already show a preference for visually fixating on a human face rather than a scrambled face and on the mother's face rather than other faces. They also appear to have some basic color, depth, and shape discrimination (Field 1990). However, the infant needs to learn to attend to and use these cues effectively, in order to develop a mature perception of depth (Rock 1975). Hence, the visual perception skills present at birth require experience to reach full expression.

Most of the lifetime development of oculomotor control occurs during the first six months of life. At first, eye movements are random. The infant's oculomotor responses are limited to momentary crude monocular fixation, visual regard, and irregular tracking of a moving light (Erhardt 1986). Visual orientation is easier in the supine position because the infant lacks head control and in this position the head is properly supported (Bly 1994). The infant at one month of age utilizes monocular fixation and tracks with the head and eyes moving together in response to a moving target. Visual pursuit occurs from the periphery towards the midline. By three months of age, the infant has developed binocular fixation and can now see her hands when they move in front of her eyes (White 1975). By six months, the infant demonstrates smooth convergence/divergence and visual accommodation and is able visually to track objects in all directions as efficiently as an adult (Erhardt 1986).

The visual system becomes increasingly more important in the human interaction with the outside environment. By the time the child is thirty-six weeks old, visual perception of space has become precise enough to allow visually guided reach to become smooth and accurate, and vision guides action (White 1975).

Vision and postural control impact each other. As the child gains postural control over upright positions, the visual field is enhanced and the hands are freed to manipulate (rather than bear weight). This in turn impacts the refinement of visuomotor skills or eye-hand coordination. Vision, proprioception, and touch also impact each other. For instance, during the early phases of visual motor development, an action such as reaching is initiated by vision but also is very dependent on proprioceptive feedback (Colangelo et al. 1976).

By integrating tactile and proprioceptive input with visual and vestibular information, the infant learns about her body—the way it feels, looks, and moves. This sense of knowing one's own body is referred to as body scheme or body percept and is defined as "body maps that are stored in the brain. These maps contain information about every part of the body, their relationships among all the parts, and all the movements each part can make" (Ayres 1979, 63). Body percept starts developing early and continues throughout the first years of life. It is an essential milestone in the development of motor planning skills, as the child first needs to learn about his body and later learns how to maneuver this body in relation to space and objects. During the first six months of life, the infant learns to coordinate her eyes and orient the head, eyes, and hands to the midline. Processing of tactile and proprioceptive input is pivotal in the development of hand skills, and the integration of this information with visual and vestibular input is necessary for the development of eye-hand coordination (see Figure 1-2 on p. 26).

The cognitive developmental milestones attained during the first six months of life depend on performing, learning from, and modifying primarily reflexive behaviors. From one to four months of age, the baby exhibits: intentional movements in that some behaviors that occurred by chance are now being repeated in order to obtain an interesting or advantageous result; anticipation, occurring as a result of associations made between sensory cues such as being held in a specific manner when being fed, the action (sucking), and the satisfaction of a need (hunger); curiosity of novel stimuli (a toy); and imitation of previously performed actions. These actions are limited to vocalizations, ocular movements, and grasping (Ginsburg and Opper 1969).

The Distinct Contribution of Sensory Processing During the First Six Months

During the first six months of life, the infant becomes more efficient at localizing and discriminating between tactile sensations and thus contributes to the development of oral motor skills, hand manipulation skills, body scheme, and the acquisition of motor planning skills (Ayres 1979). An infant plays with his hands and brings them together to the

Figure 1-2. Processing of tactile and vestibular information contributes to the parent-infant and "mother earth"-infant bonds. Observe the child's integration of sensory input; the hand is resting on the father's chest, and she rights her head and trunk against gravity while focusing on an event in the distance. Photo by Shay McAtee.

chest, his mouth, to touch his knees or feet, and finally uses them to bring the feet to his mouth. As the infant moves and touches his body, visual, proprioceptive, and tactile input from this activity are integrated to produce a unified concept of each body part and how it feels, looks, and moves. When the baby brings hands and, later, objects to his mouth, he learns to adjust the hand position to the contour of the body and thereby acquires information about his hands, body, and mouth (see Figure 1-3 on p. 27). In addition, hand-to-mouth play decreases oral sensitivity, and hand-to-foot, foot-to-mouth, and foot-to-foot play prepare the feet for future weight bearing (Bly 1983).

When the infant in the supine position brings her hands to her feet and her feet to her mouth, she also develops the abdominal musculature that allows control over flexion against gravity. Pleasure derived from the tactile experience of touching her feet probably reinforces the flexor pattern.

Integration of vestibular and proprioceptive input enables the child to assume different positions against gravity. Vestibular, proprioceptive, and visual input also influence the development of righting reactions, protective reactions, and equilibrium reactions throughout life. Children right their heads in response to gravity and later protect themselves and readjust their posture in response to vestibular, somatosensory (proprioceptive and tactile), and visual input (Shumway-Cook and Horak 1986). As the infant moves through developmental sequences, such as movement from sitting to quadruped, into kneeling, half-kneeling, and standing, she detects the force of gravity, movement of the head, and changes in the body parts in relation to each other. Processing this information is necessary for moving in space. Children who do not process this input adequately do not develop efficient postural control and are unable to adjust their bodies in anticipation of a change in their center of gravity.

Oral motor development necessary for the production of speech requires discrimination of tactile input and proprioceptive feedback. The child needs to know how to position the tongue and lips to produce the necessary sound. Children provide themselves with tactile and proprioceptive input by mouthing objects. This behavior enhances the development of adequate tactile and proprioceptive processing and contributes to the child's knowledge about the properties of objects (see Figure 1-3).

Learning to repeat previously performed actions and imitations is influenced by the processing of proprioceptive feedback. Linking a stimulus with a response requires the child to modulate the input to acquire the state of equilibrium described above, and to discriminate

Figure 1-3. Adequate processing of tactile information enables the child to habituate to grass texture and gain information from her body from hand-to-mouth and hand-to-foot exploration. By exploring the body with the hands, the child learns to contour the shape of the palm around the object. Photo by Shay McAtee.

visual, tactile and/or auditory input. Hence, at this age, in order for learning to occur, the infant needs to move from regulating his own body sensations to attending to the sensory cues in the environment (see Table 1-2 on p. 14).

Signs of Atypical Development During the First Six Months of Life

Poor modulation of sensory information may affect the infant's self-organization during basic interactions in daily life, such as cuddling, changing, feeding, and bathing. The daily routine may offer many opportunities for the infant to organize input and calm herself after being stressed. Infants who are unable to cope with the everyday care-taking routine exhibit behaviors such as crying for long periods of time after being changed, inability to calm down during feeding, and inability to maintain a regular sleeping pattern. Thus, the amount of time spent in a calm, alert state of consciousness is limited.

Signs of inadequate processing of tactile input can be observed in oral motor, fine motor, and gross motor functions, as well as social-emotional well-being. Adequate oral motor functions are pivotal in feeding. Some difficulties related to deficient tactile processing include poor rooting and sucking; difficulty transitioning to table food; poor eating patterns; and difficulty with hygienic activities that require abrupt changes in temperature, such as taking a bath.

Signs of inadequate processing of tactile input, which is primarily poor modulation, also can be observed in the baby's social-emotional development. The child may tend to become irritable or arch his back in response to being held. Later in life, these children often avoid contact with other people or interacting with objects that provide unusual tactile experiences.

In the arena of gross motor skills, decreased antigravity flexion may suggest a sensory processing deficit. Children who do not process tactile input adequately might not derive pleasure from exploring the body and feet and may not repeat this action. Decreased control over the abdominal musculature often is observed in older children who exhibit tactile processing dysfunction and may suggest an association with an earlier reduced body exploration in the supine position.

Signs of vestibular processing deficits may be evidenced by inadequate antigravity extensor control. Children who are hyporesponsive to vestibular input often exhibit poor thoracic extension accompanied by a tendency to maintain the scapulas in abduction. Scapula adduction and thoracic extension appear early in life. Poor antigravity extension results in a rounded upper back later in life. It is important to point out that none of these signs in isolation indicates a dysfunction.

The Second Six Months of Life

During the second semester of life, the infant's responses become primarily self-initiated, voluntary, and organized actions on the environment. Equilibrium reactions in the sitting position become more efficient, allowing the child to change positions and move in space. By the end of the first year, the child has evolved into a mobile, upright creature who explores space and manipulates objects (see Figures 1-4 and 1-5).

Increased mobility through space provides the infant with the opportunity to use evolving organizational skills. For example, by ten months of age, the infant is able to organize small units of social interactions and feelings into large, complex "orchestrated patterns" of behavior (Greenspan and Greenspan 1985, 5). As a result of this increased organizational skill and control over movement in space, the infant no longer cries to get her needs met but may take action, such as taking the caregiver's hand and showing him the sink because she wants water. Organizing units into orchestrated patterns of behavior is evidenced in all areas of development—motor skills, social interactions, and language.

In the arena of gross motor skills, by the sixth month of age, flexors and extensors balance each other and contribute to the infant's ability to bear

Figure 1-4. This picture captures automatic integration of many sources of sensory input and motivation to explore the environment. The child leans against the window, maintaining proximal joint stability in the shoulder girdle and trunk area. He integrates proprioceptive information from the contraction, rights against gravity by integrating vestibular information, adapts the position of the hand to the supporting surface by integrating tactile and proprioceptive information from it, and directs conscious attention to the visual information. Photo by Shay McAtee.

Figure 1-5. The child is able to lean down and grasp a toy. This task requires participation of the entire body, equilibrium reactions, fine motor/manipulation skills, and adequate processing of vestibular-proprioceptive-visual input, in order to adjust the body position in relationship to gravity. Photo by Shay McAtee.

weight on both hands, lift her head and upper torso from the supporting surface, and shift her weight from side to side (Bly 1983). Processing information about gravity and the supporting surface is pivotal for these skills to be developed adequately. During the second six months, the infant gains control of the upright position and learns to use increased motor control to move through space.

Weight bearing and weight shifting on the hands provides tactile and proprioceptive input that affects the development of the entire upper extremities and hands (see Figure 1-5). Weight bearing and weight shifting prepare the hands for future function by facilitating the development of the arches of the hands for mature grasp. Hand movements become more differentiated as the influence of primitive hand reflexes diminishes (Exner 1989).

Adequate hand manipulation requires controlled grasp and release. Controlled grasp evolves from a radial palmar grasp at about six months, through three-point prehension at about eight to nine months, to pincer grasp at twelve months (Exner 1989; Gesell and Amatruda 1974). This refinement in grasp follows a proximal-to-distal and an ulnar-to-radial sequence. Controlled release also develops during the second semester. At first, release occurs when the palm of the hand rests against a surface as when transferring objects from hand to hand. By the end of the first year, the infant is able to control release of an object free in space. Grasp and release are influenced by the refinement of tactile and proprioceptive processing (Exner 1989).

The development of bilateral upper extremity use during the last six months of the first year of life evolves from symmetry to controlled asymmetry in bilateral hand use (Exner 1989). At approximately seven months of age, the infant transfers objects adeptly from hand to hand and soon after, differentiates movements of both upper extremities during a task. These skills rely on dissociation of both sides of the body and the abilities to use both arms simultaneously (Exner 1989) and process tactile and proprioceptive input adequately.

As upper extremity control increases, so does the efficiency of manipulation. By the end of the first year, the child can grasp small objects and hold and manipulate them with both hands. The increased control of the hand is affected by early experiences with tactile and proprioceptive input. Upper extremity control now is coupled with increased oculomotor control, allowing eye-hand coordination to become more refined.

Language is influenced by the respiration pattern. At approximately seven months of age, the respiratory system, which provides the power for speech production, reaches the level of coordination between inspiration and expiration necessary for the production of words (Connor et al. 1978). Maturation of the breathing pattern is dependent upon the postural control developed earlier. This postural control was at first highly dependent on sensory input. As the child approaches the first year, he learns his first words, which signals true language learning (Gesell and Amatruda 1974).

Cognitive skills are developed during the latter part of the first year, and they include object permanence, object relations, and cause and effect (Ginsburg and Opper 1969). These cognitive skills affect language, praxis, and social-emotional development. These skills are evidenced in the capacity to have a goal before the action is started, in more systematic imitation skills, and in construction capabilities. Recognition of the relations between objects is evidenced at first by the child hitting objects in the midline, such as when dangling a ring attached to a string, and by the child attempting to put one object on top of another. Later, the infant learns to anticipate object movement and accommodate his actions to an interruption pattern (Colangelo et al. 1976; Gesell and Amatruda 1974; Ginsburg and Opper 1969).

The ability to engage in a voluntary motor act and accommodate the action in response to an interruption characterizes the second phase of self-regulation, also called sensory motor modulation (Kopp 1982). It helps infants become aware of their own actions, which will need to be differentiated from those of others, in order to develop the next phase of self-regulation—control (Kopp 1982). Control develops during the second semester and is replaced by self-control at approximately twenty-four months of age. Between nine and seventeen months of age, the behaviors associated with mastery motivation include a preference for exploration and control (Busch-Rossnagel 1997).

As the child moves in space, the sensory systems provide the information to act adaptively. The vestibular system provides information about space and direction of movement. The proprioceptive system provides feedback about the body and the type of movement performed by the body. The visual system provides information about the visual spatial arrangement, and the tactile system, in collaboration with the above-mentioned sensory systems, provides information about the body and the objects that are encountered in the environment. The integrated information provides a unified experience of movement in space.

As children learn to attend to a task for longer periods of time, they become more purposeful. Evidence of this skill is the ability to place objects into a container (Gesell and Amatruda 1974). Attending to a task requires filtering out extraneous information. Children whose CNS does not modulate sensory input adequately, respond indiscriminately to the sensory input in the external environment. Inefficient modulation of sensory input makes engagement in a purposeful task and learning more difficult for these children.

Signs of Atypical Development During the Second Semester

Atypical sensory development during the second semester can be observed in the infant's interaction with objects, weight-bearing patterns, movement patterns, oral motor control, and responses to novel stimuli. Children who are hyper- or hyposensitive to tactile and proprioceptive experiences either avoid contact with objects or do not respond to the tactile/proprioceptive information from the object being held. Lacking normal sensory input from the hand about the object, they do not respond to it adaptively.

Youngsters with tactile and proprioceptive deficits may tend to avoid weight bearing on open palms or may have difficulty adjusting the position of their feet to the supporting surface. Children who have difficulty modulating tactile input often sit and stand early in life in an attempt to reduce the body's contact with the weight-bearing surface. Other signs of inadequate tactile processing include inadequate body scheme and clumsy movements.

Irregularities in motor development that suggest motor planning difficulties include the tendency to stay in one position and avoid movement transitions, and poverty of movement patterns (Blanche 1998). These types of motor planning deficits often are observed in conjunction with decreased muscle tone and a decreased response to tactile and proprioceptive input.

Signs of oral motor deficits that suggest sensory processing deficits include difficulties with sucking, excessive drooling, poor oral motor control, avoidance of bringing objects to the mouth, difficulties with transitioning to table food, delayed acquisition of speech, inadequate chewing patterns, and avoidance of soft foods.

The tendency for sameness and lack of exploratory behaviors also may suggest a sensory processing problem as well as other types of problems. During the first nine months of life, mastery motivation is evidenced in the child's preference for novel stimuli (Busch-Rossnagel 1997). Therefore, decreased exploration may suggest atypical developmental delays.

The Second Year

The second year is characterized by an increase in the toddler's self-control. This self-control is evidenced in the motor, emotional, and cognitive areas and relies on previously acquired sensory motor skills.

Motor control becomes more accurate in that gross motor skills progress from unstable ambulation at twelve months to climbing, running, and moving through obstacles in the environment at twenty-four months of age. The child's movements are fluid and coordinated. Balance between flexors and extensors allows trunk rotation during movement, which in turn allows for mature postural control.

As mature postural adjustments are perfected, the child develops the ability to perform complex actions, such as tiptoeing, jumping, and standing on one foot. These motor skills require feedback, feedforward, and bilateral motor coordination, skills that have been linked to the development of somatosensory and vestibular input (Ayres 1979; Fisher 1991). Processing of vestibular input also impacts postural reactions and oculomotor control during actions that require maintaining a stable visual field while moving (Fisher 1991), such as when running and kicking a ball, or swinging and hitting a target.

Increased control in the fine motor area is evident in efficient, timed release of an object. Increased efficiency over object release allows for the development of skills such as building a tower, inserting small objects into a container, and doing simple puzzles.

Proprioceptive and visual feedback contribute to the ability to reach, grasp, and release. Bilateral motor coordination continues to develop and, by the end of the second year, the child establishes complementary use of both upper extremities. During an activity, each hand performs a different role and co-operates in the performance of bimanual tasks (Fagard 1990). This cooperation is observed in activities such as threading beads. The performance of bimanual tasks requires bilateral motor coordination, which is related to processing of vestibular input (Ayres 1972, 1979).

The third phase of self-regulation, control, develops during the second year. Control is characterized by the child's ability to show awareness of social demands and task demands. Being aware of the demands in the environment is evidenced by compliance with requests. This stage is referred to as control because the term implies less flexibility than regulation (Kopp 1982). Being aware of the demands in the environment depends on the ability to process sensory information from one's own body and the task at hand. Being aware of the demands of the task becomes important when the toddler changes her preference for exploration to one of challenging and goal-directed tasks. This occurs at about seventeen to twenty-two months of age (Busch-Rossnagel 1997). The child's success in meeting the demands of a challenging task is coupled with pleasure, and the inability to complete a task is coupled with sadness. Therefore, unsuccessful evaluation of the demands of the task may impact the development of self-esteem, mastery motivation, and emotional well-being.

During this time, the toddler's motor skills allow her to move away from the primary caregiver. The motor skill of moving away, coupled with the development of mental representations of absent objects or people, facilitates some limited separation from the adult (Coley 1978). Children who lack the motor ability to move away from the caregiver or who have experienced repeated failure may have difficulty developing control over the separation.

The cognitive area undergoes significant quantitative and qualitative expansion during the second year. By the end of the second year, this expansion allows the toddler to begin to solve problems at a mental rather than a motor level. At this age, cognitive processes precede action. The child develops an interest in producing new behaviors to solve new situations, such as dealing with an obstacle in new and creative ways. This is evidenced when he uses a tool to obtain a desired object, such as climbing on a chair to reach a toy (D'Eugenio 1986). Examples of more complex organized behaviors include going to the refrigerator and pointing to a desired food, or rolling a ball back and forth (Greenspan and Greenspan 1985).

At about twenty-four months of age, the toddler develops the ability to make a mental symbol stand for something that is not present. Imitation is a precursor to symbolic representations (Ginsburg and Opper 1969). The mental symbol involves visual imagery as well as body sensations arising from the previous experience with that object. The use of symbolic thought also is seen in language. At first the child uses words to refer to ongoing processes. At about two years of age, the child uses words to refer to absent objects (Ginsburg and Opper 1969). This leads to imitation of an absent model or deferred imitation (Ginsburg & Opper 1969). Deferred imitation is a step in the development of gestural representation, an element of praxis (Kaplan 1977).

In summary, cognitive development and the development of learning rely on the ability to organize sensory information into meaningful units. The ability to modulate and later discriminate between sensory input is essential to the development of cognitive skills. Increased control over the internal body environment and, later, over the external world allows organizational skills to increase in complexity.

By the end of the second year, the infant has learned to combine words into two- or three-word sentences, and tends to communicate primarily through language. The child learns not only the meaning of words but also of combinations of words (Connor et al. 1978). This ability to combine words in the use of language was preceded by the ability to combine objects and actions in the physical world.

Sensory discrimination continues to be developed during the second year and is influenced by cognitive development. Cognition attaches meaning to sensory input. In turn, adequate processing and modulation of sensory input early in life may impact the development of cognition (Ayres 1972, 1979). Processing of visual information is important in coordinated movement and the development of cognitive skills such as anticipation, intention, and curiosity. These skills in turn facilitate the development of praxis. Visual perception in conjunction with cognitive development also are important in the development of the visual discrimination skills used in matching basic shapes and colors.

Signs of Inadequate Processing During the Second Year

Signs of inadequate processing of sensory input are evidenced in deficient fine motor and eye-hand coordination skills such as inadequate weight-bearing patterns of the upper extremities, inadequate grasp patterns, poor object manipulation, and poor bilateral motor coordination. Inadequate processing of sensory input also is evidenced in the delayed development of praxis skills. Children with poor somatosensory processing skills may exhibit poor use of tools, such as a spoon or crayon; poor imitation skills, as in poorly articulated speech; poor constructional skills, as in building a tower; and poor organizational skills, as when performing a multiple-step activity. In turn, poor sensory motor and motor planning skills impact social-emotional well-being.

The Third Year

Over time the young child learns to move in space and adds complex activities such as going up and down stairs and using a tricycle, to his repertoire. At this point, vestibulo-proprioceptive input will impact not only postural control, but also coordinated use of both sides of the body; timing of the response; fluidity of the movement; and the ability to project one's own action sequences in space and time (Ayres 1972, 1979, 1989; Fisher 1991). Children who do not adequately process vestibular input show postural deficits and fear when interacting with a demanding environment. They also may appear clumsy, slow, and cautious when challenged by movement in the environment.

The vestibular and proprioceptive systems also play a role in the child's compensatory eye movements, which are eye position corrections in response to movements of the head and body (Fisher 1991). These movements begin early in life and are important for focusing on a target while moving in space. Visual, vestibular, and proprioceptive sensations provide an integrated experience of eye movements in relation to the head position and gravity. In addition, proprioceptive feedback from the oculomotor muscles provides information about the position of the eyes (Ayres 1979).

The beginning of the third year marks the emergence of self-control, which later becomes evident in the last phase of self-regulation. These two phases differ from the previous one because of the emergence of representational thinking and recall memory, both of which appear at about eighteen months of age (Kopp 1982). Self-regulation appears when the child has internalized the rules.

In terms of mastery motivation, between thirty-two and thirty-six months of age, the child begins to show a preference for challenging tasks requiring sequential ordering of multiple parts and the acquisition of performance standards. Performing the task successfully is accompanied by pride, while not achieving the task is accompanied by shame (Busch-Rossnagel 1997).

Signs of Atypical Development During the Second and Third Years

Signs of inadequate processing of proprioceptive/kinesthetic input include a lack of fluidity in movement sequences, poor proximal joint stability or ability to co-contract, poor grading of muscle force as evidenced in clumsiness, inadequate awareness of the demands of the task, and an increased tendency to lean or push on caretakers or other supports. Because proprioceptive input often has a calming effect, children who exhibit tactile modulation difficulties may also seek large amounts of proprioceptive input in an effort to modulate incoming sensory input through pushing, hitting, pinching, biting, and other behaviors that may seem antisocial.

Language has been found to relate to processing of vestibular input. Children who present a vestibular processing deficit often attain language milestones late (Ayres 1979). In addition, speech articulation requires adequate processing of tactile and proprioceptive input (see Table 1-3 on p. 17).

Mistretta (1990, 68) stated that the sense of taste may be liable "in health, disease, and altered physiological states." This liability may also be characteristic of children who have sensory processing dysfunction and exhibit unusual reactions to taste and smell. Hence, in some instances, strong food preferences and aversions may alert the adult to possible atypical development.

SUMMARY

Sensory processing is pivotal in development. The infant learns from his actions and the environment through the senses. These sensory systems provide a basic window through which the child experiences the world. Sensory input from several sources is integrated and organized to form meaningful clusters of experiences.

Performance of Daily Occupational Activities

Development of sensory, motor, and cognitive skills impacts the child's ability to perform daily occupations. This section describes the development of the performance of daily occupations including self-care and play. Examples of the impact of sensory processing on activities of daily living are illustrated in Table 1-7 on p. 37.

Emergence of Self-Care Skills

Self-help skills described in this section include feeding, dressing, and hygiene. Feeding is the earliest self-help skill to be developed, and problems in this area may indicate early signs of inadequate sensory processing. Newborns spend most of the day sleeping, and when they are awake, primarily they eat. Feeding, at this age, is impacted by neuro-

Table 1-7.   Sensory information required to perform activities of daily living*

TYPE OF DAILY ACTIVITY	SENSORY INFORMATION REQUIRED TO PERFORM THE ACTIVITY SUCCESSFULLY	OTHER COMPONENTS
Feeding		
Sucking	Tactile, proprioceptive	Oral motor skills
Holding bottle	Tactile, proprioceptive	Upper extremity (UE) motor skills, cognition (cause-effect)
Finger feeding	Tactile, proprioceptive, visual	UE motor skills, cognition
Taking spoon to mouth	Tactile, proprioceptive, visual	UE motor skills, cognition
Transferring to solid food	Tactile, proprioceptive	Oral motor skills
Dressing		
Stretching the arms inside the sleeves while being dressed	Tactile, proprioceptive, body percept, motor planning	Motor skills, cognition
Finding the arm sleeves	Tactile, proprioceptive, visual, spatial perception, motor planning	Motor skills
Pulling pants on	Tactile, proprioceptive, visual, motor planning	Postural control
Accepting garments being pulled over the face	Vestibular, tactile, visual	
Hygiene		
Washing face	Tactile	
Accepting having teeth brushed	Tactile, gustatory	
Being aware of soiled diaper	Tactile	

Reprinted with permission. (Blanche 1996)

regulation and sensory-motor regulation. Touch is an important system for gathering information from the environment. For instance, tolerance of tactile input is required to accept the handling during feeding, and basic tactile discrimination is required to distinguish the nipple from the skin surrounding it. Sucking also relies on the processing of tactile and proprioceptive input. Early signs of sensory processing and motor deficits during the first weeks of life include difficulties both with finding the nipple and sucking efficiently from it.

By the sixth month of life, rooting in response to tactile stimulation and the suck-swallow reflex have disappeared. Additionally, the bite reflex has diminished. Between six and twelve months of age, gains made in self-feeding are dependent on sensory motor development occurring in the upper extremities and the oral motor area. During this period, infants begin to eat solid food, learn to suck food from a spoon, and become proficient at feeding themselves a cracker. They also can hold a bottle and bring it to their mouths. These actions require tactile and proprioceptive discrimination, basic motor coordination, and overall increased differentiation (Coley 1978). Changes in oral motor skills occurring between six and ten months of age are the most dramatic relative to this area, throughout the developmental span. During this time, the infant learns to eat pureed food with a mature eating pattern (Gisel 1990). Also, the infant exhibits basic chewing patterns and decreases drooling (Coley 1978). During this period, signs of inadequate sensory motor skills may include prolonged time needed for eating pureed food, difficulties transitioning to pureed food, inability to close the lips around a spoon and suck food from it, and inadequate oral motor manipulation of pureed food.

The increased refinement of upper extremity use and cognitive functions occurring during this second semester of life is evident in the child's ability to bring the cracker to his mouth and the ability to hold a bottle with both hands. Inability to perform these tasks signals early signs of dysfunction.

By twelve months, the child is able to use a tool such as a spoon to bring food to her mouth. As oral motor control increases, chewing patterns continue to develop and drooling decreases (Coley 1978). By the end of the second year, the toddler has learned to feed himself with utensils and handle a cup efficiently (See Figure 1-6). These skills rely on the ability to process tactile input from holding the spoon in his hand, proprioceptive

Figure 1-6. In order to be able to eat from a spoon and drink from a cup, a child must have basic practic skills. Scooping with a spoon requires processing of proprioceptive and visual input as the child adjusts the action according to the feedback he receives. Drinking from a cup also requires adequate processing of tactile and proprioceptive input in the oral area. Photo by Shay McAtee.

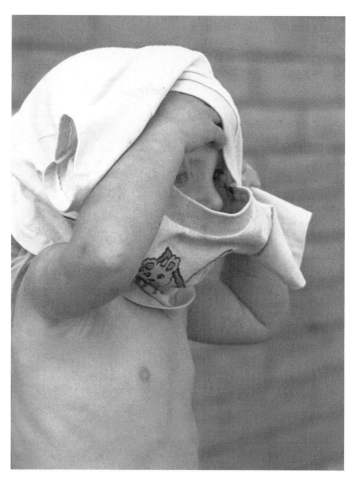

Figure 1-7. Self-dressing requires the processing of tactile and proprioceptive input to adjust the position of the clothing. It also depends on the ability to maintain a steady posture and motor plan throughout the task. Photo by Shay McAtee.

input from the movement of his hand toward the mouth, and visual input of the location of the spoon and the plate. In addition, the eating strategies used by children up to twenty-four months of age have been found to be dependent upon the texture of the food, in that solids take the longest time to chew, and puree, the least (Gisel 1991). These results suggest that the ability to process tactile and proprioceptive input in the oral area is pivotal to the development of adequate eating skills.

In dressing, the infant assists himself at first by lifting and pushing the extremities through the clothing (Gesell and Amatruda 1974). This skill reflects the ability to anticipate an outcome, motor plan in preparation for that outcome, and be motivated to gain control by finding the openings in the clothing (Coley 1978). Dressing requires basic motor planning, sensory processing of visual, tactile and vestibulo-proprioceptive input, and organization of behavior. In order to perform this task efficiently, infants need to be able to identify the position of the extremities inside the garment without using vision; they need to move the extremities in an efficient manner; and they must have basic perception of space so that they can recognize front from back and up and down (see Figure 1-7). As children continue to develop the ability to organize acts into a meaningful routine, dressing becomes more efficient. Increased organization is evidenced in the ability to sequence acts, such as putting the shirt over the head, pushing arms through the holes, and pulling the shirt down. However, dressing is a multiple-step, purposeful activity that requires organization of behavior in a larger spatio-temporal environment. For example, the child needs to organize himself to put on his underwear, pants, and socks and shoes. There is an established sequence that needs to be followed. Because dressing is a complex skill that relies on adequate sensory, motor, and cognitive abilities, its development can be affected by deficiencies in any of these areas. For instance, a toddler with inadequate tactile and proprioceptive processing skills associated with poor body scheme may have difficulty putting her head through the top of a sweater. Another child with vestibulo-proprioceptive deficits associated with poor perception of space and postural control may be unable successfully to shift his weight to one side so that he can place one foot through the pants leg. A child with practic and organizational difficulties may be unable to sequence the dressing routine successfully.

Other activities of daily living include bathing and toilet training. During the first two years of life, the child is dependent on the adult for the performance of these activities. However, the infant needs to be able to modulate sensory input adequately so that she can adjust to changes in temperature when bathed, or to being handled when placed on the changing table. Bathing requires that the infant be able to regulate the state of alertness, in spite of an abrupt change in the environment (see Figure 1-8 on p. 41). Difficulty in regulating the state of alertness may impact behavior during this activity. Changing the diaper requires placing the child in the supine position, which means a change in body position in space that may not be tolerated easily by a child who exhibits motor dysfunction or a child who exhibits gravitational insecurity. As toddlers mature, they need to discriminate tactile and proprioceptive input during a bath so that they can perform the washing action themselves. A child's inability to complete toilet training successfully may also be influenced by general muscle tone and regulation of visceral and proprioceptive sensations. Examples of how sensory processing and associated motor deficits may affect the acquisition of these self-care skills include a child with tactile hypersensitivity who may be very particular about the texture of the washcloth or about having his hair washed; or a child with low muscle tone who may have difficulty learning to control bowel movements.

Emergence of Play and Exploration

Exploration appears early in life. During the first weeks, the baby derives pleasure from tactile explorations such as bringing hand to mouth, and from visual exploration such as focusing on objects and faces in the environment. Visual exploration later is integrated with manual and oral exploration, which provide tactile information about the properties of objects. At first this occurs as children explore the hands and feet, and later as they explore objects in their hands. This combination of

Figure 1-8. The ability to adjust to different textures and temperatures allows this child to enjoy his time in the bathtub. Bathing often provides the opportunity to explore the body and develop body scheme. Photo by Shay McAtee.

movement and visual input contributes to the infant's conception of the world (Fenson 1985).

As the child gains control over gravity and movement in the upright position, she gains new horizons for social and perceptual interactions (Gesell and Amatruda 1974). For example, postural control in the sitting position frees the hands for playing with toys and interacting on a different plane. Crawling allows exploration of larger space. During the second semester (six to twelve months of age), the repertoire of play behaviors includes banging, interacting with a mirror image, and moving objects in and out of containers. Toward the end of the first year, the child's interest in small objects increases, and he becomes interested in imitating words and basic acts (Gesell and Amatruda 1974).

The child's daily routine and play behavior changes significantly during the second year. The child's movement in space and control over the environment increases and the child becomes more of a member of the culture and society in which she belongs. Play provides a view of the impact of culture on the child (Gesell and Igi 1949). Another aspect observed in play is the infant's interest in finding the cause and effect of events, which is demonstrated by the curiosity observed when playing with a wind-up toy (D'Eugenio 1986). The play repertoire expands to include pretend play and manipulative activities (Fenson 1985). During this period, most of the child's day is spent exploring rather than socializing (White 1975).

As cognitive and practic skills are developed, pretend-play becomes more complex. The child imitates a sequence of a daily routine such as putting her dolls to bed, waking them up, having them go to school, and later, having them eat lunch and then putting them back to bed (Greenspan and Greenspan 1985). Play also includes musical and other artistic activities.

Daily occupational activities including exploration and play are impacted by development in all areas. Therefore, observing a child's play behavior and toy preference provides a sample of his development. For example, children with modulation deficits often tend to explore the environment without engaging in play, while other children overfocus on only one toy and do not accept a change in that routine. Children who have constructional deficits often avoid toys that require assembling pieces, such as interlocking blocks, and instead prefer simple-action toys. Yet using toys that challenge the child's skills provides practice, learning, and enhancement of overall development. For example, assembling puzzles, constructing a tower, pushing a shopping cart, and riding a tricycle can be enjoyable activities for a child while also promoting development of higher level skills. Therefore, children who avoid challenges in their play may further hinder their own development.

SUMMARY

The ability to integrate sensory input adequately has an effect on motor, cognitive, and social-emotional development. This chapter has described three developmental concepts and related them to the theory of sensory integration:

1. The nature/nurture/culture impact on development;
2. The principle of increased organization; and
3. The principle of the child as an active agent in shaping her own development.

Understanding normal development and the impact of sensory processing on this process provides a basis for evaluation and treatment of children. Integration of sensory information allows individuals to derive meaning from the world around them. Through the senses, children learn about the world and how to function in it. The first six months in the life of a child are important as the child learns to regulate physiological and sensory motor states, acquires basic control over gravity, starts developing body scheme, and attains visuomotor control.

During the second half of the first year, children learn to move through space and relate to objects. At the same time, simple motor planning skills appear toward the last quarter. Improved postural control has increased the time spent in the upright position, freed the upper extremities for fine motor activities, and has significantly altered the sensory, motor and social interactions with the environment. The child's development expands from: exploration of objects in a semi-static sitting position to active exploration of space; simple sounds to communication through the use of words; simple environmental and social interactions to initiation of complex interactions.

Increased organization and differentiation of behavior occur during this stage. This is apparent in the qualitative and quantitative differences occurring in the motor, language, cognitive, and social areas. The increased organization facilitates basic motor planning skills, an element of praxis that starts to develop during this semester; speech and language; and social-emotional development. The appearance of praxis and its organizational process, which requires ideation, motor planning, and execution, is not fully evident until the second year.

During the second year, the toddler evolves from walking to exploring the environment and climbing on furniture. Cognitive skills become a greater moving force behind the child's actions and language. Actions are combined into organized behavior and true praxis emerges.

After twenty-four months of age, the integration of sensory input continues to impact the development of perception, language, motor coordination, social-emotional comfort, and organizational skills. These more complex skills depend upon the adequacy of the previously acquired skills. Visual perception is improved as the child now is able to match colors and simple forms. Visual skills coupled with cognitive development allow the development of copying and imitating in two- and three-dimensional modes, speech and language, and social-emotional development.

The child's quality of performance of daily occupations such as eating, dressing, and playing, indicates his degree of developmental competency, and it may reflect difficulties and delays in sensory, motor, cognitive, and social areas. The areas of dysfunction that need to be addressed in treatment may be identified by adding to the overall assessment an observation of a child's performance of daily occupations.

CHAPTER 2

Milestones Program Structure: Why, Who, What, Where, and When

Katherine Newton Inamura, M.A., OTR
Terri Chew Nishimura, M.A., OTR
Patricia S. Webster, M.A., OTR
Victoria McGuire, B.S., Ed.
Lori Shaw, M.Ed.
Zoe Mailloux, M.A.,OTR, FAOTA

The young child's development of appropriate movement patterns, body percept, form and space perception, praxis, communicative skills, cognitive abilities, play and socialization skills, and self-care skills has been shown to be dependent upon the effective use of sensory information to guide adaptive responses to daily events. Difficulty processing and integrating sensory information has been postulated to contribute to delayed and atypical development, including disorders in behavior and learning.

In addition to being one of the first to recognize the link between sensory integration and development, Dr. A. Jean Ayres was a leader in devising treatment methods based on her theories, research, and clinical experience. These sensory integrative treatment methods encourage a child's participation in activities that provide specific kinds of sensations (particularly vestibular and tactile-proprioceptive) and, in turn, enable the child to perform with more skill, ease, and complexity. The Ayres Clinic staff and many other clinicians have found the use of sensory integrative treatment techniques to be an effective one-on-one approach for numerous infants and toddlers with developmental delays. However, in the 1980s the staff of the Ayres Clinic perceived the need to create a new type of early intervention program.

Both the staff and the parents of children receiving individual treatment at the clinic believed that a group program for toddlers would be beneficial. They indicated that a group program could provide: (a) increased development as a result of more opportunities for peer interaction in a supportive environment as well as involvement in a greater variety of activities and (b) better preparation for participation in informal play groups and more structured enrichment classes. With the input from the parents in mind, the staff identified six elements for the prospective early intervention program:

1. Sensory integration theory and its treatment approach would provide a foundation for the program's design.
2. Development of the young children would be facilitated in all developmental domains.
3. The staff would be composed of members of various professional disciplines.
4. The children would have opportunities to model and interact with peers.
5. The parents and other family members would be invited to participate actively in the program and have opportunities to interact with other families.
6. The environment would be similar to community programs for children without special needs.

The Milestones program was developed to incorporate these components into an early intervention program. Over time, there have been changes to create a better fit of the environment, the staff, and the needs of the children and their families. As with any dynamic program, this is an ongoing process.

This book conveys basic information about Milestones to guide others who might wish to create a similar program or use components of this program. Naturally, no situation is exactly the same, so precise replication of the program may not be possible or necessarily desirable.

The following is an introduction to the significant values and assumptions that have guided the development of the Milestones program. These primarily are based on sensory integration theory and treatment techniques. However, other theoretical bases that are relevant to the program will be briefly presented. The remainder of the chapter describes the program's participants, routine, environment, and objects.

Theoretical Bases

Occupational therapists who select specific theories to guide their practices often are more efficient and effective in choosing activities, solving problems, and explaining the rationale of their intervention services to other professionals and patients and their families (Miller 1988; Mosey 1989; Parham 1987). The cohesiveness, collaboration, and effectiveness of the Milestones staff have been aided by the identification of particular theoretical bases to direct program development and implementation. To promote better understanding of the program, an overview of these theoretical bases is presented.

Sensory Integration

The theoretical base of sensory integration affects all aspects of the Milestones program. It influences the children selected for participation, the staff composition, staff-child interaction, environment, schedule, activities, and problem-solving techniques. This theory guides intervention with its postulates that a child with deficits in sensory processing will have difficulty achieving optimal development, but that such a child experiencing enhanced sensation during meaningful activities and having opportunities to plan and organize adaptive responses will be more likely to maximize her potential.

The following are principles of sensory integration theory and treatment techniques that are the basis for many of the decisions made regarding the program (Ayres 1972, 1979, 1985; Clark, Mailloux, and Parham 1985; Fisher and Murray 1991; Parham and Mailloux 1996). Additionally, examples are given to illustrate how these principles guide the choice and presentation of activities.

1. *The development of sensory integration occurs in an orderly sequence.* For example, a child will develop awareness of her fingers and thumb as separate units of her hand by first placing her entire hand in contact with objects and tactile materials (e.g., finger paint, rice, or carpet) and manipulating them.

2. *An appropriate amount and type of sensory input can promote adaptive responses.* By controlling the speed and direction of motion of a bolster swing being ridden by a child, the staff member enables the child to demonstrate appropriate postural responses to the motion of the swing.

3. *The production of an adaptive response aids the development of sensory integration.* The child who is successful in maintaining his balance on the bolster swing may be able to use that kinesthetic memory to maintain his balance on a rocker boat.

4. *A child often seeks the type of sensory experiences he needs.* The toddler who constantly is crashing into equipment and purposely falling from heights to the floor may require extensive deep-pressure input. The staff should help the toddler receive the intensity and amount of deep-pressure sensations needed via appropriate activities, such as pushing and pulling pieces of equipment.

5. *Effective processing of tactile, proprioceptive, and vestibular sensations contributes to appropriate processing of visual and auditory sensations, acquisition of language and academic skills, and emotional adjustment.* A child who is able to filter out extraneous visual, tactile, proprioceptive, and auditory stimulation will have better attention in a structured group setting. Reducing a child's tactile defensiveness and visual distractibility may enable her to sit still long enough to complete a simple puzzle.

6. *As much as possible, the child needs to be active in choosing and planning the activity.* First, the staff member should wait to see which piece of equipment or toy the child approaches. Then, if the child does not engage in purposeful play, the staff member should offer the child choices

about what to do with the equipment or toy. Another child may need help selecting an appropriate activity. After the selection, the staff member will need to observe the child for verbal or nonverbal cues as to the child's preferences during the activity, and adjust the activity accordingly.

7. *The staff should nurture and encourage exploration and variety.* Whenever possible, the role of a staff member should be that of a cheerleader and fellow explorer, as opposed to an authoritarian telling a child how to do an activity correctly. The staff member should encourage the child to try something slightly different or new, compliment the child on his efforts and successes, be enthusiastic about her own participation in the activities, and provide just enough assistance to facilitate the child's success.

8. *The environment and activities should be designed to facilitate exploration and success.* An enticing obstacle course for toddlers might include a short tunnel, a slide with steps, and a walking board laid on the floor. By selecting equipment that is somewhat familiar yet appropriately challenging to the children, the staff is preparing an activity and environment that will be appealing and conducive to the children's mastery of their adaptive responses.

9. *When a child achieves better organization of adaptive responses, the child's general behavioral organization will improve.* By learning to sequence and time the actions involved in climbing up the steps of a slide and then sliding down it, the toddler will in turn increase her general ability to organize her behavior. Thus, the toddler may demonstrate an enhanced ability to remain seated at the table until she has completed her snack.

10. *The overall goal of this approach is not to teach specific skills but, rather, to make the child more capable of learning.* The aim of the program is to provide appropriate sensory input that will elicit improved adaptive responses and lead to more mature and complex developmental skills (see Figure 2-1 on p. 49). For example, to foster learning to place forms on a form board, the child is provided with a wide variety of objects and materials for manipulation and experimentation.

Other Theoretical Bases

Although sensory integration theory provides the main theoretical base, other intervention approaches also are integrated into the program. These include therapeutic techniques based on the theories of neurodevelopmental treatment (NDT) and occupational behavior. In addition, concepts from Piaget's studies of cognitive development and play influence the choice and presentation of some activities. Speech and language intervention also relies on the theories of natural language and pragmatics. Finally, the overall implementation of the program is guided by the principles of family-centered care.

Figure 2-1. A child is captivated by the sensations he experiences while moving his hands through foamy soap. Photo by Shay McAtee.

Neurodevelopmental Treatment

The methods arising from NDT principles, which originally were developed by Bobath and Bobath, often are used by occupational, physical, and speech therapists with children having cerebral palsy. The overall purpose of this approach is to assist the child's acquisition of normal postural control and movement patterns. The therapist facilitates these abilities in the child by skillfully "handling" the child during purposeful activities. Handling involves the provision of graded tactile, proprioceptive, and vestibular input through key points of control (points of therapist's contact with the child's body) (Bobath 1963, 1967; Bobath and Bobath 1964).

Recently, therapists have advocated combining the treatment approaches of NDT and sensory integration in the treatment of some neurologically impaired children (DeGangi 1990; Blanche, Botticelli, and Hallway 1995; Blanche and Burke 1991). Blanche, Botticelli and Hallway indicated that the judicious use of the NDT approach in conjunction with the sensory integrative approach may be helpful in addressing the aspects of a child's movement dysfunction related to alignment, postural stability, and movement patterns.

Within this program, NDT techniques are used with children who demonstrate immature or abnormal postural control and movement patterns. The staff uses these techniques to facilitate normal postural control and movement patterns during actions such as mounting and dismounting equipment, riding therapy equipment, walking, eating, and drinking. For instance, a therapist may stop a bolster swing at an angle to allow a child with emerging equilibrium responses to make appropriate postural adjustments to her body's changed relationship to gravity. The therapist may use the child's pelvis as a key point of control to facilitate a realignment in her trunk. In a different situation, a therapist may facilitate a child's initial movement to mount, bolster by shifting the child's weight from the supporting right leg on the mat to the child's left knee placed on the bolster.

Occupational Behavior and the Emerging Science of Occupation

The theory of occupational behavior based upon the work of Mary Reilly (1974) emphasizes the importance of occupational role. Occupational role can be considered a developmental sequence of player, student, worker, and retiree. The period of childhood is viewed as crucial for learning, exploring, and developing rules and skills about people, places, objects, and abstract concepts. Through exploration, appropriate activities, and practice, a child develops competency. Competency in learning these early tasks is necessary for later adult performance of occupation roles (Florey 1971; Reilly 1974; Robinson 1977). Play in its various forms provides a major means by which young children acquire the experience and knowledge necessary for competent interaction with the people and objects in their world (Mack, Lindquist, and Parham 1982).

These tenets influenced the original design and selection of activities for this program. The Milestones environment is structured to be similar to a "play group" setting. The program strives to provide opportunities for learning skills, habits, and rules through play. For example, the children have the chance to explore playing with several sizes and types of balls. As a result, they develop skill in handling the balls; discover which balls are good for throwing, rolling, or kicking; and learn the social rules concerning ball play. With respect to self-care, the children are encouraged to practice skills and develop habits relative to putting on and removing socks and shoes, washing hands, and self-feeding. Additionally, they are exposed to the social rules of sharing and taking turns. Furthermore, the young children have opportunities to act out social roles such as being a cook, a shopper, or a birthday party participant. The staff views the neurodevelopmental treatment approach and sensory integration treatment techniques as complementary to the occupational behavior approach because the facilitation of a child's proficiency in neuromotor skills and sensory integration will increase the child's competency as a player. The child will be motivated to explore and master environmental challenges and enhance self-organization as she participates in play and self-care activities.

Around the time of Milestones' initial development, occupational science was being defined and introduced as an innovative academic discipline (Clark et al. 1991; Clark and Larson 1993; Yerxa et al. 1990). This new science focuses on the study of humans as occupational beings and, in turn, their occupations. Occupations are proposed to be purposeful, culturally defined, and personally relevant units of activities that may hinder or aid a person's successful adaptation to environmental challenges. Clark et al. (1991) postulate that occupations are the result of (a) a complex interaction of physical, biological, information processing, social-cultural, and other subsystems; (b) the human drive for competency and effectiveness; (c) influences of a person's present circumstances and past; and (d) an individual's values. Parham and Primeau (1997) suggest that current and future studies of play as an occupation will reveal new findings concerning the intertwining of play and work, the influence of play on adult occupations, and the importance of "competent" play to promoting health.

Milestones, with its emphasis on family involvement and promotion of various types of play within a peer group environment, supports the concept of play as a complex occupation having value as a therapeutic tool for many aspects of development. Milestones and other early intervention programs will need to incorporate information resulting from new research about play into their program designs.

Piagetian Theory

The contributions of Piaget and his associates to theories about cognitive development and play should be considered by those who work with children. Piagetian theory stresses the importance of the child's active interaction with her world (Gruber and Voneche 1977; Phillips 1969; Piaget and Inhelder 1969; Pulaski 1980). The child learns by her sensory experiences and by her motor actions. During the child's sensory motor exploration of her body and environment, she organizes and adapts her internal mental structures and external physical actions.

These postulates make a Piagetian-based approach compatible with a sensory integration-based approach. Piaget proposed that during the first two years of life, a child develops concepts of object permanence, object properties, spatiality, and causality (Gruber and Voneche 1977; Phillips 1969; Piaget and Inhelder 1969). According to Piagetian theory, a child learns object permanence as he realizes that an object continues to exist although he cannot see or touch it. During exploration of toys and household objects, the child discovers the physical properties of objects (e.g., size, shape, malleability) and that objects can be spatially related to each other and the environment (e.g., put inside one another, rolled on the floor, turned over). As part of this process, the child learns about means-ends relationships or how to use an intermediary object to achieve a desired result (such as pulling on a blanket to bring a toy closer). The child also becomes aware of cause-and-effect relations or what makes certain things happen and how to use adults to make these events happen.

Piaget and his associates indicated that a child progresses through developmental sequences relative to imitation and play. The first level is based on the child's sensory motor experiences. The second level emerges with the child's ability to use language and mental representations of objects and their relationships. The child develops increasingly complex ways of interacting with objects, people, and the environment.

The Milestones staff's awareness of these aspects of Piagetian theory has influenced the selection of toys to aid in the child's discovery of cognitive concepts; for instance, pop-up toys for cause-and-effect (understanding what makes things happen), pull toys for means-ends (understanding how to make something happen), and nesting cups for spatial relations. Knowledge of the developmental progression in concept formation, imitation, and play has helped the staff to direct activities to the appropriate levels of the child's development. For example, the staff recognizes that a child will imitate waving and saying "bye-bye" inexactly before performing exact imitations, play simple peek-a-boo games before finding a toy hidden under one of two cups, and simply practice putting blocks in and out of a bucket before pretending the bucket is a pot and the blocks are food.

Pragmatic Language and Natural Language Approaches

In addition to the previously described theories, the speech and language intervention of the program has been influenced by the pragmatic and natural language treatment approaches. Pragmatic language theory stresses that there are both verbal and nonverbal components of language needed for social interaction (Bloom and Lakey 1978). The nonverbal and verbal elements include the appropriate use of eye contact, gestures, posture, tone of voice, turn-taking, and words as well as phrases for social acknowledgment, requesting, answering, and continuing a conversational topic.

Natural language theory indicates the importance of facilitating expressive (produced by oneself) and receptive (produced by others) language within the context of everyday events, including play (Hatten and Hatten 1981). Adults can promote language development by modeling appropriate language, encouraging imitation of language, and expanding on the child's language relative to naturally occurring situations. Thus, the child's use of pragmatic language can be fostered as part of a natural learning program. Examples of how these approaches are integrated into the program include having the children request more food by words or gestures, requiring turn-taking to put pictures on a felt board at Circle Time, and modeling the use of words instead of hitting to express anger.

Family-Centered Care

One of the reasons for creating this program was to provide greater opportunities for the staff and families to work as a team. Family-centered care is the provision of services in such a way that the parents and/or other family members are an integral part of the service team (Grady 1989;

Hanft 1989; Vincent 1989). The involvement of families is necessary and desirable because a child requiring medical, therapeutic, and/or special educational services does not exist in isolation, but is part of a family. Infants and toddlers are particularly dependent upon their families for survival and nurturance. The family unit has a major influence on the efficacy of intervention services. In family-centered care, the focus of intervention shifts away from just providing direct services to the child to fostering the ability of the family to facilitate the development of their child through their own and the community's resources (Dunst, Trivette, and Deal 1989; Vincent 1989).

Family-centered care in early intervention is guided by the following principles:

1. The family, not the service provider, is the ongoing source of support for the child.
2. Families are diverse in structure, roles, values, beliefs, strengths, and coping styles. These elements are influenced in part by a family's racial, ethnic, and cultural background.
3. Service providers should inform families thoroughly and impartially about their child's needs and care.
4. Service providers should respect the autonomy of the family in decision-making with respect to services and goals.
5. Collaboration between families and professionals, as well as between professionals and agencies, is essential to comprehensive care.
6. Services should be provided in as normal a manner and environment as possible.
7. The provision of services should be flexible, accessible, and responsive to family needs.
8. Interaction between families of children with special needs encourages the development of support networks. (Dunst, Trivette, and Deal 1989; Grady 1989; Vincent 1989)

Significant support for family-centered early intervention services was gained by passage of the Education of the Handicapped Act Amendments of 1986, Public Law 99-457. This legislation added Part H, which provides limited funds to those states that have chosen to create and expand comprehensive services for infants and toddlers experiencing or at risk of experiencing developmental delays.

In 1990, Congress passed additional Education of the Handicapped Act Amendments, Public Law 101-476, which changed the name of the act to the Individuals with Disabilities Education Act (IDEA). Part H, which covered early intervention services, was implemented in October 1993 in California (implementation varied by state). IDEA was reauthorized and amended in 1997 with the passage of Public Law 105-17. The section governing the provision of early intervention services was retained but now is Part C of this law.

In response to implementation of Part H of IDEA in California, the Ayres Clinic made more formal and standard the already existing process of collaborating with families. Following are details on how families can become involved in the program.

Participants

In the Milestones program, there are three major groups of participants: the children, their families, and the staff members. This section will identify the children and their special needs, discuss the family's options concerning degree of involvement, and specify the staff members and their roles.

Children and Their Special Needs

In each community there may be a variety of referral sources, including pediatricians, independent health-related professionals, neonatal follow-up programs, state or private agencies, and families. The majority of referrals to Milestones are made by the lead state agency responsible for providing prevention services to children at risk for experiencing developmental delays and early intervention services for children with existing developmental disabilities. This agency has state funds to pay for these services. Children who are referred by their parents or by other professionals and do not meet the criteria for receiving services from the state agency may participate in the program if the family is able to pay for these services through insurance coverage or other means.

In the geographic area of the Ayres Clinic, there was the greatest need for an early intervention group program to service children with mild to moderate developmental delay. Other programs were serving children with greater developmental delays and disabilities. The philosophy of the major referring agency was that the provision of intervention services for most children younger than eighteen months of age should be in the home setting. Because of these factors, the original Milestones groups were geared toward the higher-functioning, older toddlers. However, with some modifications in activities, schedules, and staffing, a sensory integration-based program could be designed for a younger or lower-functioning group.

Diagnoses

The children who are referred to the program have a variety of diagnoses, including cerebral palsy, developmental delay, autism, prematurity, prenatal drug-exposure, and congenital syndromes such as Down syndrome and Fragile X. However, the children are not referred on the basis of diagnosis but based upon the presence of developmental delays. Often they have problems that may be related to poor sensory integration and praxis. Examples of these problems are tactile defensiveness, limited attention span, fear of movement, and stereotypical play behavior (e.g., repeatedly lining up toy cars in a row).

Entrance Criteria

The entrance criteria specify that the children should be (a) fifteen to thirty months of age, (b) at risk for experiencing developmental delays or displaying mild to moderate developmental delays (e.g., developmental skills that are three to twelve months behind chronological or adjusted age), (c) walking independently or at least pulling to a standing position, and (d) able to tolerate a multisensory group program. Typically, the referred children are demonstrating delays in achieving developmental milestones or skill performance of inadequate quality relative to the following domains:

1. *Sensory awareness and ability to adapt to sensory stimulation.* A number of the children entering the program have under- or overresponsiveness to the sensations of touch, position, movement, gravity, taste, smell, sight, and/or hearing.

2. *Praxis.* Many have difficulties with one or more areas of praxis, such as ideation (having ideas about how to play with toys or large pieces of equipment), planning (deciding how to move the body to carry out a desired activity), or execution (carrying out the actions with the correct sequence, timing, and coordination).

3. *Organization of behavior.* Probably more than half the children have insufficient initiation, attention, persistence, adaptability, and emotional stability. Thus, they have difficulty playing appropriately in a group setting or attending to leader-directed activities.

4. *Gross and fine motor skills.* Most children are displaying delays in these skills. Some children are still unstable in walking and others need to work on hand skills for manipulation and tool use (e.g., crayons and spoons).

5. *Language and communication.* Almost all of the children have some degree of delay in this domain. Some rarely make any vocalizations and are not even using gestures for communication. Others are using one or two words but have a limited vocabulary with respect to the number and kinds of words.

6. *Cognitive and perceptual skills.* Most of the children have some delays in developing mental concepts about the relationships between body, objects, and environment. For example, a child may lack color or shape recognition, be unable to identify body parts, or not understand that pushing the button makes the toy figure pop up.

7. *Play organization and social skills.* Some of the children play with toys in an immature way (e.g., just mouthing, banging, or throwing the toys). Other children move quickly from toy to toy, never really playing in a purposeful way with the toys. Still others play with only a few toys in repetitive ways such as spinning toys, bouncing balls, or moving a car back and forth.

With respect to socialization, some children have great difficulty leaving their mothers' sides to play. Others seem rather oblivious to the presence of peers. A few are very aggressive toward peers and/or adults.

8. *Self-help skills.* A number of children have inadequate feeding skills. The children also may have difficulty in learning initial dressing skills. The problems may be related to fine motor skills, eye-hand coordination, spatial perception, or behavior. Additionally, parents frequently express frustration with their attempts to toilet train the older toddlers.

The staff is able to be somewhat flexible in applying the entrance criteria. In some cases, children accepted into the program are demonstrating delays greater than twelve months in some developmental domains. Additionally, a child who is not walking independently may be able to attend the program if a parent or another caregiver accompanies the child. Because the staffing and activities are geared toward children who are able to walk, the presence of a partner for the child ensures the safety of that child and enables maximum participation by that child.

When a child's behavior during the preliminary visit indicates that he or she may not be ready for participation in a group program, the child may be accepted provisionally. After a trial period of two to three weeks, the program director will talk with the family and case manager. A joint decision will be reached about whether continued participation in the group program would be appropriate. If it is agreed that the program does not best meet the needs of the child and family, alternative services will be discussed.

Exit Criteria

A child's participation may be discontinued if he meets any of these four criteria:

1. Child's or family's needs will be better met by a different program;
2. Infrequent attendance;
3. Achievement of age-appropriate developmental skills; or
4. Attainment of three years of age.

Sometimes after a child has begun the program, the family and staff determine that the family and/or child has needs that are not sufficiently addressed by the program. After consultation with the family and case manager, a transfer to another program or other services (such as individual treatment) may take place. For example, a child having a low functional level, hyperresponsiveness to sensory input, or medical fragility may be unable to function in this type of group program. Such a child may respond better to intervention in the home setting or to individual treatment in the clinical setting.

Another possible reason for termination from the program before age three is infrequent attendance. The child's discharge may become necessary if there is a waiting list for the program and the child's attendance remains very inconsistent in spite of discussion with the child's family and case manager. Additionally, a child may be discontinued from the program before age three because of the consistent performance of age-appropriate behaviors, or a child may be discharged at age three with nearly age-appropriate skills.

The majority of children who enter the program continue participation until they reach three years of age, which is the maximum age. Over the length of their participation, the children demonstrate significant progress with respect to the domains identified in the section on entrance criteria. Some specific examples of possible gains are included in the discussion of sensory integration theory and treatment principles earlier in this chapter. Other examples are increased tolerance of food textures, imitative ability, attention to verbal and manual direction, standing balance, use of words, matching of shapes, varied play with the same toy, turn-taking ability, and cup-drinking skill. Improvements in these abilities and skills help prepare children to be more independent and to participate in community play groups and preschool settings. Although these children have shown definite progress in decreasing the amount of developmental delay, often they are still demonstrating a significant degree of delay and qualify for programs offered by a public school or state agency.

Group Fluidity

Because Milestones is a year-round program, children may begin participation at any point in the year and end participation whenever they have reached the age of three or demonstrate age-appropriate developmental skills. Therefore, the program population changes frequently. Because of the variance in developmental levels and the fluidity of the group's membership, the program curriculum has to be individualized and cannot be based on the assumption that all group members will be participating for the same period of time.

It is easiest to maintain a group's ease of routine if only one or two new children begin at the same time. However, it is not always possible to stagger the entry of new children as far apart as would be desirable to keep the group's stability. For example, several openings in the group may occur in quick succession during autumn due to the transition of older children to school-based programs.

Families and Their Involvement

As indicated earlier, family involvement is critical to the success of an intervention program. The family-child relationship is the foundation for all aspects of development. However, flexibility regarding the degree of involvement of parents in the program is necessary because of the varying needs of families. Requiring attendance of a family member or caregiver with each child may severely limit the number of children able to participate. On the other hand, excluding families from active participation or ongoing observation of the program may interfere with the desire of some families to have frequent, direct collaboration with the program's personnel. These family members may wish to learn how better to promote their child's development.

Program staff include the parents as members of the team while recognizing that each child and his family is unique in their needs and values. The program uses a number of ways to involve the parent as decision maker and participant. Regular parental participation is encouraged but not required.

Introduction to the Program

Usually, the case manager from the state agency will make the first contact with the program director to initiate a referral. If possible, a family member and the child will visit the program prior to deciding about enrollment. During the visit, the family member is able to see the physical environment, toys, and equipment. He or she meets the staff, children, and attending parents. Also, the family member is able to observe the program's routine and activities and the child's reaction to the group program. The staff shares with the family member the philosophy and goals of the program, the rationale for the routine and particular activities, and the staff composition/ratio. The staff gives this information verbally and in written handouts (typically the first three items indicated in Table 2-1).

At the time of this initial visit, the staff is able to observe the child's level of function and interactions with the other children and staff. The staff considers whether the child seems ready for a group program, is functioning at a level compatible with those of other children, or is more likely to benefit from individual therapy or another type of group program. Placement in the program is based on the mutual agreement of the child's parents, the case manager, and the staff.

Upon the child's enrollment, the parent receives a packet containing additional information about the nature and services of the clinic and program, clinic policies regarding appointments and financial responsibility, and forms for the parents to complete and return. Table 2-1 lists some of the material contained in the parent packet. A clinic director gives the parents an orientation, usually on the first day of a child's participation. The orientation includes a tour of the facility, a brief overview of the history of the clinic and treatment approaches, and a review of the forms in the parent packet. The program director and staff

Table 2-1.   Suggested items for parent packet

Facility Mission Statement and Fact Sheet

Sensory Integration Information Sheet or Booklet

Program Description and Fact Sheet

Program Parent Handbook (see Appendix A)

Child and Family Information Questionnaire (see Appendix B)

Consent for Release of Information

Consent for Emergency Medical Treatment

Family Perspective Questionnaire (see Appendix C)

complete the orientation by providing the parents with the necessary information unique to Milestones (such as the Program Parent Handbook, see Appendix A) and by answering any questions.

Usually by the time the child begins the program, the staff will have received from the referring case manager relevant psychosocial, medical, and developmental information, including reports of previous intervention services (such as in-home therapy) and developmental evaluations. Because the state agency customarily has conducted at least one developmental evaluation of the child to determine eligibility for service, the staff does not generally give another developmental assessment at the time of program entry.

Shortly after the child begins the program, the director or other staff member will meet with the family to discuss the child's current level of functioning and the family's needs and concerns. (See Appendix C for examples of the types of questions that may be used to guide the interview.) During the interview, the staff member and family collaborate on establishing goals and objectives for the child's first six months of participation. (The process for setting and documenting goals and objectives will be discussed in Chapter 5.) The staff uses the information from the referring agency and parent interview, as well as observations of the child, to guide interactions with the child and with family members.

Participation in the Program Sessions

Although the staff invites regular involvement, parents choose their own degree of participation in the program sessions (see Figure 2-2 on p. 60). Typically, parents have varying degrees of participation within a given day or over the months that a child attends the program. Some parents do not attend the program at all or attend only infrequently because of work outside the home, the care of other children, or other responsibilities. In some of these cases, a grandparent or other caregiver may attend with the child.

Over time, the parents who attend the program sessions with their children become acquainted. If the parents are observing during the Exploratory Play period, they often talk informally at that time. Some parents choose to sit and talk in the adjoining waiting room. Frequently, the parents share information, concerns, resources, and solutions relative to their children and their lives. A time for more structured discussion is provided in the parent group meetings.

Collaboration with Staff

By participating in the decision to enroll a child in the program, the parents begin collaborating with the staff to provide the most appropriate intervention services for their child and family. Through the initial interview and other discussions, the parents provide pertinent information about their child's and family's strengths, areas of concern, and daily routine. The staff members share their observations about the child and make suggestions about how to foster the child's development.

Figure 2-2. In the security of his mother's lap, a child enjoys exploring a pool of balls. Photo by Shay McAtee.

In addition, the staff uses bulletin boards, handouts, and monthly newsletters to keep families informed and promote collaboration. The newsletters describe the concepts being emphasized each month, report staff changes, announce parent meetings and other significant events, and suggest home activities. Upon a parent's request, the staff will give an individualized written description of activities that can be performed at home.

During the monthly parent meetings, the parents, family members, and staff have an opportunity to share ideas as a group. The meetings, which last about forty-five minutes, are held during the program session in a room separate from the children. Each meeting is planned around a specific topic such as sensory processing, praxis and motor development, cognitive development, speech and language development, discipline, play and socialization, and transitioning to public school. Customarily a staff member serves as the group leader and makes a brief presentation about the topic. Occasionally a guest speaker is invited. Together the group leader and family members discuss the topic.

Sometimes parents express an interest in assisting during the sessions with the administration of the program or clinic. The staff may ask these parents to help with some clerical tasks, preparation for arts and crafts, or setting out the snacks.

When a child is ready for discharge from the program, the staff, along with the case manager, assists the family in preparing for this transition. In order for a child to be discharged at age three, a transition meeting is scheduled for when the child is between thirty and thirty-three months old. In addition to the parents and the program director, the child's case manager and a local school district representative (if appropriate) participate in the meeting. The child's progress is reviewed and the parents' concerns are discussed. If it is decided that formal evaluations are needed, the case manager and school representative will establish which institution will conduct the evaluations. The program options provided by the school district will be presented. Arrangements will be made for the family to visit the various programs.

The transition process will be somewhat different for the family of a child who is being discharged with age-appropriate developmental skills or with needs that will be better met by other services. The parents, case manager, and program staff member may meet before the child is thirty months of age if the discharge is to be sooner. Information about the child's participation in the program is shared with the parents, the child's case manager, and other professionals as requested by the parents. Other possible services and community options are discussed. The family may observe other intervention services available at the clinic or at other facilities before choosing a course of action.

Staff Members and Their Roles

The professional identity of the staff for an early intervention program often is determined by a variety of factors, including the population being served, the availability and interest of particular professionals, and the requirements of funding sources. As discussed earlier in this chapter, Part C (formerly Part H) of IDEA emphasizes the importance of participation by members of different professional disciplines in the provision of early intervention services. The professionals may apply their expertise to early intervention programs in ways ranging from periodic assessment and consultation to daily involvement.

Team Members

The Milestones program is staffed to provide at least one staff member for every three children. The maximum number of children enrolled per group has increased from twelve to sixteen. The size of the staff has been adjusted accordingly from four to six members present during a program session.

Staffing includes occupational therapists, speech-language pathologists, teachers, physical therapists, and assistants. At times, volunteers or graduate-level occupational/physical therapy students assist with the groups. Their presence reduces the staff/child ratio even further. The occupational therapists, physical therapists, and speech-language pathologists have advanced training in sensory integration theory and treatment approaches. The other staff members have received an orientation to this theoretical base.

Team Approach

The staff strives to collaborate with each other, the families, and other involved agencies or schools. During much of each program session, the children, family members, and staff members are together in the same area. Most of the time, the staff members are not assigned to work with particular children but instead are free to facilitate the productive activity of any child. Typically, each child has several periods of one-on-one attention from different staff members over the course of a session. Lower-functioning children receive a greater amount of individualized attention from the staff than do children requiring less direction. During an interaction with a child and/or family member, the staff member naturally draws on his own knowledge and experience relative to his profession but also attempts to incorporate ideas and techniques learned from other disciplines.

For example, an occupational therapist might work with a child on object permanence and manual form perception (recognition of an object through feeling) by hiding a blue toy in the sand for the child to find. At the same time, the therapist might encourage color recognition and understanding of receptive language by directing the child to find the blue toy, or promote speech production by having the child imitate saying *blue*. In a similar fashion, the teacher, when presenting the concepts of *in* and *out*, might have the child place objects of different textures and shapes in and out of a container upon his verbal command. Thus, the teacher would be facilitating the child's tolerance of various textures and manual form perception in addition to teaching the concepts of *in* and *out* and their corresponding words.

The professional staff members have differentiated roles for planning and leading activities (described in the next section) and for administering tests. However, they and the assistants share their observations of the children before writing weekly notes and progress reports. The staff also jointly plans the weekly program activities.

For direct intervention and as a resource to other staff members, the speech-language clinician draws on her specialized knowledge of oral motor skills, pre-speech vocalization, communication, expressive and receptive language, and auditory perception. She administers the Language portion of the *Early Intervention Developmental Profile* (Rogers and D'Eugenio 1981; Rogers et al. 1981).

The teacher contributes her knowledge of school readiness skills, cognitive development, receptive and expressive language, and motor development. She assesses the child's skill on the Cognition section of the developmental evaluation.

The occupational therapist shares his knowledge of sensory integration and praxis, normal and abnormal development, play, socialization, and self-care skills, including feeding. He administers the Perceptual/Fine Motor, Social/Emotional, and Self-care portions of the evaluation, and also may administer the Gross Motor section of the assessment.

The physical therapist draws on her knowledge of normal and abnormal motor skills, movement patterns, and muscle tone. When appropriate, she makes suggestions to parents and staff about the positioning and handling of a child. When available, the physical therapist administers the Gross Motor section of the developmental assessment.

The positions of assistant are filled by individuals with at least a high school education and three months of experience working with children. The assistants, along with the rest of the staff, help set up the day's activities and clean up afterward. Throughout the program activities, the assistants promote the children's productive participation. Volunteers and graduate students function in a similar way as do the assistants, but the students gradually assume more professional responsibility.

Routine

When things are going well in a group, a comfortable but lively rhythm is created. Such a rhythm is a feeling that the activity level (degree of busyness) is changing in predictable, manageable patterns. The rhythm of an early intervention program session is influenced by the setting, children, parents, staff, and routine of activities. A change in any one of these factors can create a change in the dynamics of the group that affects the sessions' rhythm for better or worse. The loss of a comfortable rhythm to the sessions for an extended period may mean that some adjustments need to be made in regard to the environment, schedule, type of activities, or role of people involved. (Management of the group is discussed in detail in Chapter 4.) The routine or progression and type of activities as structured by the schedule have a particularly strong influence on rhythm. Three factors that contribute to Milestones' routine of activities are monthly concepts, session groups, and the daily schedule.

Monthly Concepts

Each month, certain concepts are targeted for special reinforcement. Generally, the concepts include a color, shape, and spatial relation. For example, the concepts for the month of October might be *orange, circle, clothing names,* and *in/out.* As the weekly schedule is planned, these concepts guide the choice of special activities, toys, equipment, songs, and snacks. The staff even makes an effort to wear clothing of the particular color and encourages parents to dress their children in the month's color on certain days. The staff tries to use every available opportunity to reinforce the monthly concepts as well as other appropriate concepts.

Session Groups

When a child is enrolled in the program, she is placed in a group of children attending the program sessions at set times and on set days (two or three days per week). This inclusion in a specific group enables the child and family to become familiar with the other children and their families and to build relationships more quickly. The regularity in the session days, times, and participants appears to help the children adjust to being in a structured, group environment and to follow the program's routine. Some exceptions may be made to the groupings, such as placing a child in a three-day group although she only attends two days a week. Another example would be allowing a child from a two-day group to come also on a day for the three-day group.

Depending on demand, the early intervention program staff may find it feasible to have more than one group of children and families attending sessions each week. For example, at times, three groups of children have taken part in the program. One group met on Mondays, Wednesdays, and Fridays from 9:30 a.m. to 11:30 a.m. Another group met at the same time on Tuesdays and Thursdays. The third group met on Mondays, Tuesdays, and Thursdays from noon to 1:30 p.m.

As indicated earlier, the maximum size for Milestones groups was raised from twelve to sixteen children. In addition to increasing staffing, changes in the program schedule (described next) were made to accommodate the greater number of children.

Daily Schedule

The daily schedule has evolved to meet the needs of the children and their families and to promote the best flow for the group sessions. Two schedules for the morning sessions that have been used successfully in the program are presented in Figures 2-3 and 2-4. The sequence and organization of the activities vary somewhat between the two schedules, but the overall routine is very similar. The afternoon sessions use the same time intervals and progression of activities as depicted in Figure 2-4.

To simplify the discussion, Schedule 2 (as shown in Figure 2-4) is used as a main point of reference for the following description of time periods, activities, and goals. (See Appendix D for an example of a schedule for a particular week.) This description of the daily schedule illustrates two formats that have been effective in implementing the overall goals of this early intervention program. Because of the particulars of staffing, environment, and population, other programs may find it advantageous to structure the time periods differently and offer other types of activities.

Exploratory Play

As the children arrive for the session, they are assisted in removing their shoes and socks. Bare feet provide better awareness of foot placement and traction for climbing. The children are directed to place their socks and

12 children/3 staff members

9:30–10:00	Exploratory Play
10:00–10:15	Circle Time
10:15–10:45	Centers (3 daily):
	Sensory Motor Integration
	Cognitive/Language
	Oral Motor/Tactile (alternate days)
	Pre-Speech/Language (alternate days)
10:45–11:00	Snack Time
11:00–11:25	Gross Motor Play/Exploratory Play
11:25–11:30	Going Home Routine

Figure 2-3. Daily Schedule 1

16 children/4 staff members

9:30–10:00	Exploratory Play
10:00–10:45	Centers (4 daily):
	Sensory Motor Integration
	Pre-Speech/Pre-Feeding
	Cognitive/Language
	Gross Motor/Language
10:45–11:00	Movement to Music
11:00–11:15	Snack Time
11:15–11:30	Circle Time

Figure 2-4.   Daily Schedule 2

Figure 2-5.   Exploratory Play. A child puts the pieces in a puzzle that he selected from the toy cabinet. Photo by Shay McAtee.

shoes in their individual baskets. Because this first time period is loosely structured, the children may choose from a variety of toys in an open toy cupboard (see Figure 2-5) or books in the book area. Another activity choice may be a simple art or craft activity, such as finger-painting a pumpkin shape or stringing a macaroni necklace. Often there is a small pool containing a tactile material such as uncooked rice or shredded paper (see Figure 2-6) available for the children to explore. Sometimes, selected toys are placed on the tables, or an imaginary play situation, such as a store, is set up. These activities are chosen to provide the children with opportunities to work toward the goals listed in Table 2-2 on p. 67.

Some children lack the necessary organization of behavior or developmental skills to engage in extended purposeful activity with toys, books, or craft materials. These children benefit from an initial play period involving gross motor movements in an adjoining room. This room is the site for the Sensory Motor Integration Center, and it contains suspended equipment such as swings and a container filled with plastic balls.

If the children lack self-initiation, they are encouraged but not forced to participate in the various available activities. They are guided verbally and physically in their interactions with materials and with people on an as-needed basis.

Centers

The centers provide a structure and time for more focused stimulation of neurological processes and skills relative to sensory processing and integration, praxis, motor abilities, cognition, speech, and language. When the group size is sixteen children, there are four centers each day. The children are assigned to one of four small groups. When the maximum number of children is twelve, three centers and three small groups are used. An attempt is made to balance the small groups so that each group contains at least one child who has some speech and one or more children who are able to remain seated and attend to activities without much prompting.

Figure 2-6. Exploratory Play. Two children show individual ways of learning about the tactile medium of dried beans. Photo by Shay McAtee.

Table 2-2.   Goals for children during Exploratory Play period

Adjust to being in a group setting

Adjust to separation from their caregivers (if that occurs)

Adjust arousal level

Self-initiate exploration of toys

Experience a variety of tactile activities

Practice perceptual motor and fine motor skills

Increase attention span and persistence at tasks

Engage in imaginary play

Develop cognitive skills

Increase child's interest in books

Practice listening and speaking skills

Participate in parallel and interactive play

Practice putting toys away

The small groups perform activities at each center for about ten minutes before moving to the next center. When there are four centers, each group alternates being at a center requiring sitting with one permitting more freedom of movement. The centers include:

1. *Sensory Motor Integration.* Two staff members lead these activities. Ideally, one of them is either an occupational or physical therapist with advanced training in sensory integration theory and treatment techniques. This training enables the leader to observe carefully each child's responses to the sensory experiences and motor/behavioral challenges, and then adjust the prepared activities appropriately. More so than in individual sensory integration intervention, the leader is somewhat constrained by the time limit and the need to divide attention among the children. However, the selected activities are those commonly used in individual treatment sessions (e.g., those that provide a variety of motion, tactile, and proprioceptive stimulation and require motor planning). Also, the activities typically involve adaptive responses of the whole body and/or gross eye-hand coordination (see Figure 2-7 on p. 68). Examples include climbing up a series of bolsters, swinging on a platform swing, jumping into a container of small balls, and throwing balls at a target. The center leaders facilitate the children's responses in order to achieve the goals identified in Table 2-3.

Figure 2-7. Sensory Motor Integration Center. Two children enjoy pulling jointly on the bar to propel the platform swing. Photo by Shay McAtee.

Table 2-3.   Goals for children at Sensory Motor Integration Center

Improve processing and integration of visual, tactile, proprioceptive, and vestibular stimulation

Improve body percept

Improve automatic postural responses

Improve overall muscle tone

Increase joint co-contraction

Increase motor planning skills

Improve sitting, standing, and walking balance

Increase strength of hard grasp

Improve gross eye-hand coordination

Develop specific gross motor skills such as jumping and walking up/down steps

Increase knowledge and use of action words

Increase interactive play

2. *Pre-speech/Pre-feeding*. At this center, there is a strong emphasis on developing the oral motor skills necessary for facial expression, talking, feeding, and drinking. However, the scope of activities is broader, extending to the facilitation of other associated developmental abilities. When Schedule 1 is followed, these activities are carried out at two centers, each with a little different emphasis. On alternate days there is an Oral Motor/Tactile Center and Pre-speech/Language Center with activities conducted by an occupational therapist and speech-language clinician, respectively.

Under Schedule 2, activities at the Pre-speech/Pre-feeding Center are directed either by an occupational therapist or speech-language clinician. Whether Schedule 1 or 2 is followed, both staff members use activities involving tastes, textures, shapes, colors, blowing, facial expressions, tongue/lip/jaw movements, and gestures (see Figure 2-8). The speech-language clinician also promotes the children's ability to attend to, produce, understand, and respond to gestural and spoken language. He may use sound toys, picture cards, books, and representational objects (e.g., toy dishes and figures). The occupational therapist frequently presents activities involving tactile stimulation of the hands and mouth,

Figure 2-8. Pre-speech/Pre-feeding Center. A child is intent on blowing a cotton ball out of a blowpipe. Photo by Shay McAtee.

and requiring adaptive responses including manipulation, object recognition, straw drinking, cup drinking, and chewing. The aim of these activities is to promote the children's development relative to the goals listed in Table 2-4.

3. *Cognitive/Language.* The teacher leads the group in activities that include matching, looking at pictures, listening to rhymes and stories, and following verbal commands (see Figure 2-9 on p. 71). Her tools may include books, picture cards, manipulative toys, and representational objects. By participating in this center's activities, the children enhance their abilities relative to the goals stated in Table 2-5 on p. 71.

4. *Gross Motor/Language.* Frequently, a speech-language clinician or occupational therapist is one of the two leaders of this center. The staff members emphasize the use and understanding of language (action words and monthly concepts) as the children play on and with equipment requiring large movement patterns (see Figure 2-10 on p. 72). The equipment may include a balance beam, rocker boat, slide, merry-go-round, balls, or wheeled toys. The staff selects activities to promote abilities included in the goals for the Sensory Motor Integration Center (see Table 2-3) and particularly to develop capacities identified in Table 2-6 on p. 72.

When Schedule 1 is followed, a combined Gross Motor/Exploratory Play period takes place during the last half hour of the program session. Approximately half of the children interact with the equipment in the

Table 2-4.　　Goals for children at Pre-speech/Pre-feeding Center

Increase attention span and in-seat behavior

Improve tolerance for various textures, tastes, and smells

Increase tactile discrimination

Improve body percept (especially of face and mouth)

Improve imitative ability

Increase oral motor skills needed for facial expression, eating, drinking, and speech

Improve auditory perception

Improve turn-taking ability

Increase sound production and word utterance

Improve gestural communication (including sign language)

Increase ability to recognize and label everyday objects, shapes, colors, body parts, and common actions.

Improve ability to follow one- and two-step verbal commands

Figure 2-9. **Cognitive/Language Center. A child looks at a reflection of himself wearing a red hat while two other children wait for their turns.** Photo by Shay McAtee.

Table 2-5.   Goals for children at Cognitive/Language Center

Increase attention span and in-seat behavior

Learn to recognize and label colors, shapes, spatial relationships, and objects

Increase ability to match objects with pictures

Improve ability to imitate gestures, sounds, and words

Improve auditory reception, sequencing, and memory

Follow one- or two-step verbal directions

Experience activities involving object permanence, means-ends, cause-effect, and visual memory

Gross Motor area while the other half engage in activities in the Exploratory Play area. About midpoint in time, the children switch places.

Movement to Music

For the Movement to Music period, the children gather in a circle with the staff interspersed around the group. Usually the parents in attendance sit with their children. One staff member leads the group in performing movements to songs and/or instrumental music. The two selections often include traditional ones such as "Ring Around the Rosie," "Hokey Pokey," or "Motor Boat." The goals of this time period are specified in

Figure 2-10. Gross Motor/Language Center. Three children challenge their motor skills by climbing on a structure. Photo by Shay McAtee.

Table 2-6.   Goals for children at Gross Motor/Language Center

Improve sitting, standing, and walking balance

Improve gross eye-hand coordination

Develop specific gross motor skills such as jumping and walking up/down steps

Increase recognition and use of words for spatial relations, shapes, colors, and actions

Increase interactive play

Table 2-7.   Goals for children during Movement to Music period

Increase awareness of body parts and their names

Improve ability to imitate simple body actions

Improve ability to move body parts rhythmically

Increase ability to follow a verbal command

Improve auditory sequencing and memory

Table 2-7. After Movement to Music (or after Centers in Schedule 1), the children wash their hands in preparation for having a snack. If Schedule 1 is being followed, the Movement to Music activities are incorporated into Circle Time, which is the second time period for that schedule (see Figure 2-3 on p. 64).

Snack Time

A snack is served to the children, who are sitting in chairs at tables or in chairs with trays. The usual snack consists of juice, finger food, and/or spoon food. The children are encouraged to eat and drink independently (see Figure 2-11), but are assisted if necessary. Some children use open cups and some use cups with spouts. Sometimes the children drink from straws in order to further develop oral motor skills. Foods and drinks of a variety of textures, smells, and tastes are served over the course of a month. The staff members attempt to facilitate better oral motor skills by hands-on intervention and consultation with parents. The children are encouraged to verbalize or use signs to indicate their desires. In addition to providing the children with needed nourishment, Snack Time offers an opportunity for the children to develop their abilities as listed in Table 2-8 on p. 74. If Schedule 1 is being used, the children participate next in the Gross Motor/Exploratory Play period. If Schedule 2 is being followed, the children are assisted in putting on their socks and shoes.

Circle Time

The children sit in a circle on carpet pieces or in chairs with tray tables. Again, the parents in attendance are usually with their children. Staff members position themselves around the circle. One staff member leads the group in singing songs and saying rhymes that involve simple body actions and other responses from children (see Figure 2-12 on p. 74). Two children select songs from illustrated sheets depicting favorites such as "Wheels on the Bus," "Old McDonald," "Head, Shoulders, Knees, and Toes," and "The Barney Song." The group also may perform another song

Figure 2-11. Snack Time. A child alternates between finger feeding and self-feeding with a spoon. Photo by Shay McAtee.

Table 2-8.   Goals for children at Snack Time

Increase willingness to eat various textures and types of food

Improve oral motor skills

Increase self-feeding and drinking skills

Increase social communication

Improve turn-taking ability

Figure 2-12.   Circle Time. Mothers encourage their children to perform the motions of an action song. Photo by Shay McAtee.

or rhyme selected to reinforce certain words or name recognition. Occasionally, other activities, such as playing musical instruments, are performed at this time.

At various times, the children are prompted to respond individually. For example, a child may be asked to identify a picture of an animal, point to a particular body part, make an animal sound, or name a toy or object brought from home. Table 2-9 on p. 75 delineates the purposes of the songs, rhymes, and other activities of this part of the program.

Under Schedule 2, a good-bye song is sung at the end of Circle Time and the children leave the session. Under Schedule 1, Circle Time follows the Exploratory Play period and is the first structured time period of the program. In that circumstance, the Circle Time activities would additionally include the Movement to Music activities. The good-bye routine of putting on shoes/socks and singing the good-bye song would occur during the last five minutes of the program session.

Table 2-9.   Goals for children at Circle Time

Increase attention span and in-seat behavior

Improve turn-taking ability

Improve auditory sequencing and memory

Increase ability to follow verbal commands

Increase sound production and word utterance

Increase understanding of monthly concepts

Increase awareness of body parts and their names

Improve imitation of simple body actions

Increase awareness of self and others as separate beings

Improve name recognition for self and others

Prepare for the end of the session (Schedule 2)

Environment and Objects

The ideal environment for an early intervention program would be one that could be designed and set up just for that purpose. It would contain a snack preparation and clean-up area, a restroom adapted for toddler use, a diaper changing area, an evaluation room, an informal meeting area for parents, a room structurally sound for suspended equipment, a storage area, and a staff work area.

Additionally there would be a very large room or adjoining small-to medium-size rooms in which various types of activities could be set up and performed. Finally, there would be an outside area for riding toys and toddler-size playground equipment, and for play with sand, water, and balls.

Most programs do not have the luxury of the ideal environment. Fortunately it is possible to create a very good program in a less-than-perfect environment. At the least, the program requires an area for suspended equipment and a space for tabletop activities. Under the best circumstances, the staff of an early intervention program would have access to numerous and varied toys, equipment, and materials suitable for facilitating all areas of development. But a program can begin with limited resources in this regard. More toys, equipment, and materials can be added as the budget permits. The furniture requirements are less extensive. Tables, chairs, and cabinets fulfill the most basic needs. Once obtained, this furniture will last for years.

Space, Furniture, and Arrangement

The Milestones program uses a waiting room, large multipurpose room, restroom, treatment room and adjoining small room on a daily basis (see Figure 2-13 on p. 77). The large room (approximately $42' \times 21'$) is divided into two areas by a playhouse, cabinets, and mat wall. The cabinets are on wheels and can be moved easily to accommodate particular activities or other programs. The mat wall folds and can serve as a gate, allowing access from one side of the room to the other. The mat wall is used because commercial child safety gates cannot be secured to the moveable cabinets.

In the front portion of this main room is a door to the adjacent waiting room. This door serves as the entrance for the program. Near this door is a bulletin board on which is posted the daily schedule and monthly concepts. The waiting room has couches, chairs, and reading materials about children with and without special needs.

Close to the entrance is an open cabinet with cubbyholes. Each cubbyhole contains a basket personalized with a child's name and photograph. The child's jacket, other personal belongings, art projects, and notices for parents are placed in these.

The front portion of the room is used for the Exploratory Play period, Snack Time, and the Pre-speech/Pre-feeding Center. During the Exploratory Play time, one toy cabinet is left open and has shelves at appropriate heights to enable the children to reach toys themselves. A large area rug is placed on the floor in front of the cabinet to provide a soft, warm surface on which the children may play. Nearby, a book area is set up with a book cabinet, rug, and beanbag chairs. Children may work on pre-reading skills and have some quiet, less active time (see Figure 2-14 on p. 78). The book area may be moved inside the playhouse on days that the playhouse is not used for an imaginary play center. A short distance away are two long tables and numerous chairs of toddler height. Craft activities or other tabletop activities are performed there. A few adult-size chairs are provided for the times when the parents are observing their children rather than actively interacting with them.

The materials and equipment for the Pre-speech/Pre-feeding Center may be placed on top of a cabinet near the tables. A couple of chairs with attachable trays are available for children who have difficulty remaining seated during the activities. More of these chairs may be used at Snack Time, Circle Time and in the Cognitive/Language Center.

The other portion of the main room is the site of Circle Time, Movement to Music, and the Gross Motor/Language Center. Storage cabinets, file cabinets, a small refrigerator, and desks line the perimeter of the room, leaving the center area free for program activities. Mats are placed on the floor as needed. At the far end of the room is the restroom. There is a sink for children and staff to wash their hands and a toilet for the children who are undergoing potty training. A nearby second restroom can be used when the number of children in attendance is large.

The Sensory Motor Integration Center activities are carried out in an adjacent treatment room. This room is specially designed with beams to

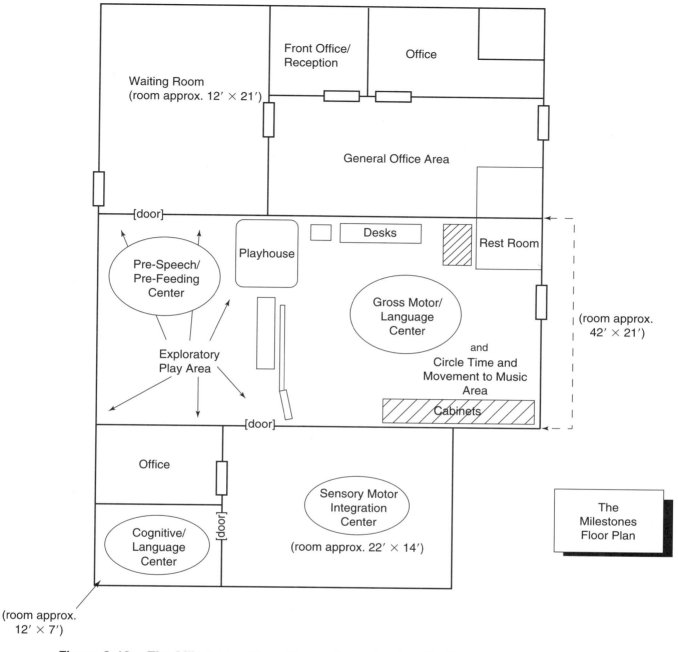

Figure 2-13. The Milestones Floor Plan. Computer Graphic Illustration by Pamela Suzuki.

support a variety of suspended equipment. The floor is covered with thick mats. There is a one-way mirror through which parents can observe their children from the main room. A small room leading from the treatment room is used for the Cognitive/Language Center and administration of portions of the developmental evaluation. A toddler-size table and chairs are available in the room.

Figure 2-14. A child studies the pictures of a book in the book area. Photo by Shay McAtee.

Equipment, Toys, and Materials

Some of the toys in the child-accessible cabinet and in the book area are taken out each month so that new ones can be brought in to maintain the novelty for the children. Periodically, other novel toys may be placed out on the tables. The types of toys include ones for manipulation, construction, and sound production. Others help the children learn object permanence, cause-and-effect, means-end, symbolic representation, visual memory, shapes, colors, and sizes. Examples include shape sorters, a surprise box, interlocking blocks, cardboard bricks, animal sound toys, pop beads, nesting cups, puzzles, a jack-in-the-box, toy cars, toy animals and people, toy houses, toy telephones, and large beads for stringing. Books also reinforce the concepts of shapes, colors, and sizes as well as depict everyday objects and activities. There are toys and objects for imaginary play scenarios such as cooking, mealtime, child care, dress-up, and shopping. In addition to variously textured toys, different tactile media are used periodically (e.g., rice, macaroni, sand, cornmeal, play dough, colored foam soap, and finger paint). A plastic sheet is placed under the pool to collect the macaroni, rice, or other tactile material spilled outside the pool. Arts and crafts projects require supplies such as paint, paintbrushes, different kinds of paper, glue, scissors, and crayons. These are also used to promote the development of expressive and receptive language.

Bound carpet pieces are used at Circle Time to designate tangibly the space where the child is to remain seated. Songbooks, tapes/records of music and songs, and a cassette player/record player are resources for the Movement to Music and Circle Time periods. Many recorded songs are paced too quickly for the children to respond. For that reason, special sheets with the words to a number of popular songs, along with corresponding illustrations, should be made. From these sheets, a child can select a song for the group to sing. A flip chart is used to display the words of unfamiliar songs for the adults. On the flannel board the children may mount pictures of items mentioned in the songs and rhymes. Occasionally, musical instruments, a hand-held shatterproof mirror, or a toy microphone may be used.

The centers require additional books, photograph cards, nursery rhyme posters, sentence strips with short rhymes, and interest-evoking objects (e.g., objects of particular color, sound-producing toy animals, and puppets). Toothbrushes, small hand-held massagers, food, blow toys, bubbles, straws, photographs of facial expressions, scrub brushes, and a shatterproof tabletop mirror are examples of other useful equipment and supplies.

While most of the toys and materials mentioned above are purchased specifically for the Milestones program, many of the larger pieces of play equipment for the Sensory Motor Integration and Gross Motor/Language Centers are shared with the other clinic programs. Among this play equipment is a large variety of swings: flexor swing, chair swing, platform swing, hammock swing, and tire swing. Other commonly used items are balls, a climbing structure, tunnels, foam blocks and wedges, bolsters, a child spinner toy, trapeze bars, a rocking boat, a merry-go-round, and a scooter board. Equipment specifically obtained for the Milestones program includes various riding toys (scooters and tricycles), a slide, a soft trampoline with a hand bar, and a push cart.

Foods and drinks for Snack Time are selected for their nutritional value, compatibility with the monthly concepts, texture, consistency, taste, and smell. Common choices include juices, milk, yogurt, canned and fresh fruit, crackers, vegetables, cheese, pudding, breads and, occasionally, cakes and cookies. Often a tray is used to serve the snack. Depending upon the items being served and the individual skill levels, the children are provided with napkins, clear plastic cups with a textured surface or cups with spouts, small plastic bowls, and toddler-size spoons and forks. The dishes and utensils are chosen for their developmental appropriateness and availability to parents. Occasionally, a special utensil or cup is required by a child. A food grinder may be used to prepare foods for children having difficulty transitioning to textured food. A basin is used to collect the dirty dishes and napkins at the end of Snack Time.

Additional program equipment includes a vinyl-covered mat for changing diapers; a toilet seat adapter; steps to the sink; a full-length, shatterproof mirror; bulletin boards for parent and staff information; and easels for painting and display of materials. Other necessary items are name tags, diaper changing supplies, disinfectant, spare clothes, paper towels, hand washing soap, dish washing supplies, and evaluation kits.

SUMMARY

This chapter has described the basic structure of Milestones, an early intervention program based on sensory integration principles. To supplement the information in Chapter 1, an overview of the sensory integration treatment approach and other theoretical frameworks has been provided to answer the query of "why" in regard to program design and implementation. The questions of who, what, where, and when have been addressed by information detailing the program's participants, environment, and routine. The next chapter contains descriptions of numerous activities that have been effective in eliciting the children's interest and enthusiasm, and in turn, developing their capabilities.

CHAPTER 3

Activities

Editors
Katherine Newton Inamura, M.A., OTR
Patricia S. Webster, M.A., OTR

Contributors
Tina M. Botticelli, M.S., PT
Julie Andersen Ewald, M.A., OTR/L
Kayra Emmons, M.A., OTR
Katherine Newton Inamura, M.A., OTR
Kirsti Kela, B.A. Speech Therapy (Finland)
Elisabeth Knauss, M.A., OTR
Corinne Koba-Moody, M.A., OTR
Victoria McGuire, B.S. Ed.
Terri Chew Nishimura, M.A., OTR
Patricia S. Webster, M.A., OTR
Nancy Wolfinger, B.A.

This chapter contains examples of activities that have been used with success in the Milestones program. These activities have engaged the children's interest and fostered their development. The 55 activities are described to aid others in selecting a beginning repertoire of activities for a program.

Although an activity often promotes a child's development in more than one developmental domain, each activity was placed into a category according to the primary developmental domain being challenged. However, if the presentation or focus of a particular activity is changed, the activity could be used mainly to enhance development of a different category of abilities than that in which it is listed. The four categories are: Sensory Motor, Cognitive/Language, Socialization/Organization of Behavior, and Self-care.

Following this page is a chart listing the activities according to category, and identifying the developmental abilities the activities may foster when presented in the manner described. The activities are listed in the category and order that they appear on the following pages. This chart can be used as a quick reference to assist selection of an activity in order to facilitate certain developmental abilities.

The next pages are the activity descriptions. Each description details the method of presentation, objectives for the children, and needed equipment/supplies. Additionally, there are suggestions for the staff on how to ease the presentation, modify the activity for a child experiencing difficulty, and adapt an activity for a child who is ready for novelty or greater complexity.

There are fewer activities listed for the Socialization/Organization of Behavior category than for the others. That is because development of skills from this category relies less on the child's experience performing particular activities than on the manner of presentation, program routine, and environment. It is hoped that the descriptions of the sample activities will suggest how other activities can be presented to enhance socialization skills and organization of behavior.

Figure 3-1 Activities and Developmental Abilities Enhanced by Them*

ACTIVITIES	Vestibular Processing	Proprioceptive Processing	Tactile Tolerance/Perception	Taste/Smell Tolerance	Body/Self-Awareness	Imitation	Postural Integration/Equilibrium Responses	Gross Motor Coordination	Oral Motor Function	Visual Attention/Perception	Auditory Attention/Perception
Sensory Motor											
1. Magic Carpet Ride	✔	✔	✔				✔				
2. Bolster Swing	✔	✔					✔	✔			
3. Inner Tube Bounce	✔	✔					✔	✔			
4. Tot Trek		✔					✔	✔			
5. Inner Tube Walk		✔			✔		✔	✔			
6. Trampoline Jumping	✔	✔			✔		✔	✔			
7. Obstacle Course	✔	✔	✔		✔		✔	✔			
8. Mountain Slide	✔	✔	✔		✔		✔	✔			
9. Ball Pool	✔	✔	✔		✔		✔	✔		✔	
10. Tactile Tunnel		✔	✔		✔						
11. Toy Grab Bag			✔		✔					✔	✔
12. "Open, Shut Them" Song With Gloves			✔		✔	✔				✔	✔
13. Finding Hidden Toys			✔		✔					✔	
14. Play Dough Fun		✔	✔		✔					✔	
15. Building With Blocks						✔				✔	
16. Blowing Fun					✔	✔			✔	✔	✔
17. Blowing Like the Wind					✔	✔			✔	✔	
18. Tongue Gymnastics		✔	✔	✔	✔	✔			✔		
19. Tasting Party			✔	✔	✔	✔			✔		
20. Smelling Party				✔							✔

***Developed by Patricia S. Webster and Katherine Newton Inamura.**

Spatial Perception	Eye-Hand Coordination/ Manipulation	Praxis	Concept Formation	Picture/Object Association	Indicating Needs/Desires	Receptive/Expressive Vocabulary	Following Directions	Imagination/Creativity	Taking Turns	Interactive Play	Following Routine	Making Choices	Feeding	Dressing	Grooming
		✓													
		✓				✓									
										✓					
✓		✓													
✓		✓													
✓		✓							✓		✓				
✓		✓									✓				
	✓	✓	✓								✓				
		✓													
	✓		✓			✓	✓		✓						
	✓	✓				✓	✓								
	✓						✓								
	✓		✓	✓		✓			✓			✓			
✓	✓	✓	✓				✓	✓	✓	✓	✓				
		✓					✓								
		✓					✓								
							✓				✓				
							✓				✓				
						✓	✓	✓			✓				

continued

Figure 3-1 Activities and Developmental Abilities Enhanced by Them

ACTIVITIES	Vestibular Processing	Proprioceptive Processing	Tactile Tolerance/Perception	Taste/Smell Tolerance	Body/Self-Awareness	Imitation	Postural Integration/Equilibrium Responses	Gross Motor Coordination	Oral Motor Function	Visual Attention/Perception	Auditory Attention/Perception
Cognitive/Language											
21. "Where is _____?" Song					✔	✔					✔
22. Feather Touch			✔		✔	✔					✔
23. Animal Names and Sounds					✔				✔	✔	✔
24. Matching Picture and Object					✔					✔	✔
25. "Stop" and "Go" Game					✔						✔
26. Forgotten Rhyme										✔	✔
27. Action Songs					✔	✔		✔		✔	✔
28. Words for Play					✔						✔
29. Shell Game										✔	✔
30. Big and Little Boxes					✔					✔	✔
31. Touching Hot and Cold			✔								✔
32. Circle Grab Bag			✔							✔	✔
33. *Brown Bear, Brown Bear Story*										✔	✔
34. Sharing Toys From Home					✔					✔	✔
35. Feeding a Baby Doll						✔				✔	✔
Socialization/Organization of Behavior											
36. Tactile Pool			✔		✔					✔	
37. Telephone Buddies						✔					✔
38. Ball Play in Pairs					✔		✔	✔		✔	✔

Spatial Perception	Eye-Hand Coordination/Manipulation	Praxis	Concept Formation	Picture/Object Association	Indicating Needs/Desires	Receptive/Expressive Vocabulary	Following Directions	Imagination/Creativity	Taking Turns	Interactive Play	Following Routine	Making Choices	Feeding	Dressing	Grooming
						✔			✔		✔				
✔			✔			✔	✔		✔						
			✔			✔	✔	✔	✔						
			✔	✔		✔	✔								
			✔		✔	✔	✔		✔	✔		✔			
				✔		✔					✔				
		✔				✔	✔				✔				
			✔			✔	✔								
			✔			✔	✔		✔						
✔			✔			✔	✔		✔						
			✔			✔	✔		✔						
✔	✔		✔			✔	✔		✔						
			✔	✔		✔	✔	✔	✔						
			✔			✔	✔		✔		✔				
	✔	✔				✔	✔	✔	✔				✔		
	✔				✔	✔		✔	✔	✔		✔			
					✔	✔		✔	✔	✔	✔				
✔	✔	✔			✔	✔	✔		✔	✔	✔				

continued

Figure 3-1   Activities and Developmental Abilities Enhanced by Them

ACTIVITIES / DEVELOPMENTAL ABILITIES	Vestibular Processing	Proprioceptive Processing	Tactile Tolerance/Perception	Taste/Smell Tolerance	Body/Self-Awareness	Imitation	Postural Integration/Equilibrium Responses	Gross Motor Coordination	Oral Motor Function	Visual Attention/Perception	Auditory Attention/Perception
39. Dollhouse Play										✔	✔
40. Pretend Play Centers					✔	✔				✔	✔
41. Nesting Cups						✔				✔	✔
42. Transition Songs					✔	✔					✔
43. "All Done" at Snack Time											
Self-Care											
44. Scooping and Pouring Play		✔								✔	✔
45. Spoon Feeding					✔				✔		
46. Chewing and Biting		✔	✔	✔	✔				✔		
47. Cup Drinking		✔	✔						✔		
48. Straw Drinking					✔				✔		
49. Paper Doll Dressing					✔	✔				✔	✔
50. Clothing Name Game					✔	✔				✔	✔
51. Socks and Shoes Practice					✔	✔				✔	✔
52. Dress-Up		✔	✔		✔	✔				✔	✔
53. Hand Washing		✔	✔		✔						
54. Baby Doll Bath			✔		✔	✔				✔	✔
55. Teeth Brushing			✔	✔	✔	✔			✔		✔

Spatial Perception	Eye-Hand Coordination/Manipulation	Praxis	Concept Formation	Picture/Object Association	Indicating Needs/Desires	Receptive/Expressive Vocabulary	Following Directions	Imagination/Creativity	Taking Turns	Interactive Play	Following Routine	Making Choices	Feeding	Dressing	Grooming
✓	✓	✓	✓			✓	✓	✓		✓		✓			
	✓	✓	✓		✓	✓	✓	✓	✓	✓	✓	✓	✓	✓	✓
✓	✓	✓	✓			✓		✓			✓				
						✓	✓				✓				
					✓	✓			✓		✓	✓	✓		
✓	✓	✓				✓		✓	✓	✓		✓	✓		
✓	✓	✓											✓		
		✓											✓		
✓	✓	✓											✓		
		✓											✓		
✓	✓	✓	✓	✓		✓	✓		✓					✓	
			✓	✓		✓	✓		✓		✓			✓	
✓	✓	✓	✓			✓	✓			✓				✓	
✓	✓	✓	✓		✓	✓		✓	✓	✓		✓		✓	
	✓						✓		✓		✓				✓
	✓	✓			✓	✓	✓	✓	✓	✓	✓	✓			✓
	✓	✓					✓				✓				✓

SENSORY MOTOR
Activity 1: Magic Carpet Ride

Lay the blanket on the mats. Direct the child to lie either on her abdomen or back, or sit in the middle of the blanket. Pull the edge of the blanket so that the child is moved over the mats.

OBJECTIVES
- Experience deep-pressure stimulation throughout the body;
- Improve motor planning required to position body on blanket; and
- Improve sitting balance.

EQUIPMENT/SUPPLIES
- Large blanket
- Uneven surfaces, such as mats

SUGGESTIONS
- Vary the speed of motion from slow to moderately fast.
- Pull on the blanket in a way that periodically changes the direction of motion.

SENSORY MOTOR
Activity 2: Bolster Swing

Have a child straddle one end of a bolster swing. Instruct the child to hold on to the supporting rope with both hands. Sit behind the child. Gently begin linear motion of the swing in a forward-and-backward direction. Depending on the child's level of confidence and automatic postural adjustments, support the child at the hips with your hands to facilitate appropriate movement of the lower trunk with the swing's motion. Use your feet to stop the swing periodically and then resume swinging. Once the child's postural adjustments are fairly good, use your hands over the child's hands to help him learn how to pull on the rope in order to help propel the swing. Increase the speed and distance traveled as the child's postural reactions become reliable. Use language to describe what the child is experiencing (e.g., "stop," "go," "swinging," and "pull"). Encourage the child to say these words.

OBJECTIVES

- Improve processing of vestibular stimulation;
- Improve processing of proprioceptive stimulation;
- Enhance postural adjustments and equilibrium reactions;
- Improve motor planning; and
- Increase knowledge and use of action words.

EQUIPMENT/SUPPLIES

- Bolster swing
- Floor mats

SUGGESTIONS

- Familiarize a fearful child with the swing by instructing him to stand on the mats and push it with his hands. Eventually, have him lean onto the swing until his upper body is supported and moves with the swing while his feet remain on the mat.
- For a child who is ready for more challenge, make the swing move side to side or in an orbital pattern.
- Have a child ride the swing alone or with another child sitting behind him.
- Suggest a pretend situation and together sing an appropriate song; for example, "Row, Row, Row Your Boat" for a boat ride.
- Have the child remove one hand from the rope and take a ball from your hand (when you have dismounted the swing).

SENSORY MOTOR
Activity 3: Inner Tube Bounce

Place an inner tube on a mat. Depending on the size of the inner tube, instruct three or more children to sit on the inner tube with their feet on the inside of the tube and bearing their weight. Encourage the children to hold hands and bounce up and down while sitting. Sing songs that involve moving up and down.

OBJECTIVES
- Improve processing of up-and-down movement stimulation;
- Improve balance responses;
- Increase proprioceptive awareness of legs;
- Improve weight-bearing ability of legs; and
- Increase interactive play.

EQUIPMENT/SUPPLIES
- One large inner tube
- Floor mats

SUGGESTIONS
- Have an insecure child place his hands on the inner tube.
- Use your hands to apply downward pressure through the hips of a child having trouble bouncing.
- Use handling techniques to counteract a child's tendency to move into an abnormal posture of adduction and internal rotation of the legs.

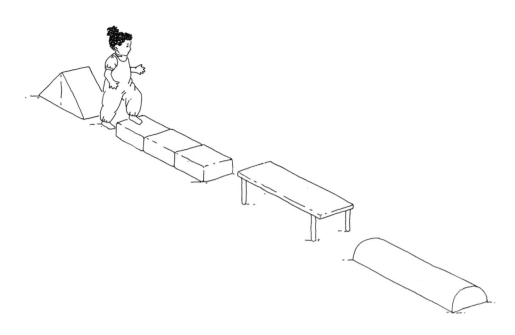

Activity 4: Tot Trek

Arrange the wedges, benches, blocks, and half rolls on the mats to create an obstacle course. Have the child walk on the equipment to follow the course.

OBJECTIVES
- Improve ambulation on irregular surfaces;
- Improve motor planning; and
- Enhance equilibrium reactions.

EQUIPMENT/SUPPLIES
- Wedges, benches, large blocks, and half rolls
- Floor mats

SUGGESTIONS
- Simplify the activity by holding the child's hand.
- Start out by using only a few pieces of equipment and gradually adding more.
- Make a game out of the trek by pretending to go to visit a friend or go to the store.
- Rearrange the equipment to provide variety.

SENSORY MOTOR
Activity 5: Inner Tube Walk

Arrange inner tubes horizontally in a pattern on the mats (in a row, a diamond shape, etc.). Place suspension ropes on hooks above inner tubes. Have the child walk across the inner tubes while holding the suspension ropes for support.

OBJECTIVES

- Increase proprioceptive awareness through upper extremity traction and lower extremity compression;
- Improve ambulation over uneven surfaces; and
- Improve balance reactions.

EQUIPMENT/SUPPLIES

- Three to five large inner tubes
- Suspension hooks
- Two or three suspension ropes
- Floor mats

SUGGESTIONS

- Use large inner tubes to reduce the chance of overturning.
- Simplify the activity by allowing the child to hold your hand instead of using the ropes.
- Include this activity as part of an obstacle course.

SENSORY MOTOR
Activity 6: Trampoline Jumping

Have children jump on the trampoline one at a time. Stand next to the trampoline while each child is jumping. Play some recorded music with a steady, moderate beat in order to set the pace.

OBJECTIVES
- Improve balance reactions;
- Improve processing of vestibular stimulation; and
- Increase proprioceptive awareness of lower extremities.

EQUIPMENT/SUPPLIES
- Small circular trampoline (no more than one foot high off the floor) or trampoline with attached bar
- Cassette player
- Cassette tape

SUGGESTIONS
- Use a trampoline with a surface soft enough for the children to have success at jumping.
- Place your hands on the child's hips and alternate applying downward and upward pressure as the child attempts to bend the legs and jump.
- Have a child who is unsteady on her feet grasp a bar or one side of a plastic hoop that you are holding as she jumps.
- Have the child recite a simple rhyme or phrase as she jumps.

SENSORY MOTOR
Activity 7: Obstacle Course

The equipment is arranged in a circuit so that the children will naturally go from one piece to another. For example, the ladder is laid flat on the floor between the slide and the tunnel. The tunnel leads to the steps for the slide. Thus, a child climbs up the steps of the slide, goes down the slide, walks by placing the feet either on or between the ladder rungs, crawls through the tunnel, and begins the circuit again. Each child waits her turn to proceed through a portion of the obstacle course.

OBJECTIVES

- Improve processing of vestibular stimulation;
- Improve processing of tactile and proprioceptive stimulation;
- Enhance body percept;
- Improve equilibrium reactions in climbing, walking, and crawling situations;
- Enhance motor planning involving weight shifts, changes in body position relative to gravity, placement of arms/legs, and timing/sequencing of actions; and
- Improve turn-taking.

EQUIPMENT/SUPPLIES

- Small portable slide
- Ladder
- Carpeted tunnel
- Floor mats

SUGGESTIONS

- Decrease balance demands by holding the child's hand while she climbs the slide steps or steps on or over the ladder rungs.
- Stabilize the tunnel for a child afraid of its rocking motion.
- Have the child's parent call out from the other end of the tunnel if the child is hesitant to enter.
- Vary the number and pieces of equipment in the obstacle course in order to change the sensory input and motor planning/skills development.

SENSORY MOTOR
Activity 8: Mountain Slide

Arrange the bolsters and wedges as shown beside the large enclosure of balls. Surround the area with floor mats. Instruct the children to creep or walk over the "mountain" and slide into the "lake" of balls in the sitting or prone position.

OBJECTIVES

- Improve processing of vestibular stimulation in a variety of body positions;
- Enhance processing of tactile stimulation;
- Enhance motor planning; and
- Improve balance reactions.

EQUIPMENT/SUPPLIES

- Four to five bolsters in increasing sizes
- Two small wedges
- Large triangular foam shape
- Large enclosure filled with balls
- Floor mats

SUGGESTIONS

- Stabilize the legs or hips of a child having difficulty crawling up the "mountain."
- Hold the hand of an unstable child walking over the bolsters.
- Rearrange the equipment to provide a different challenge.

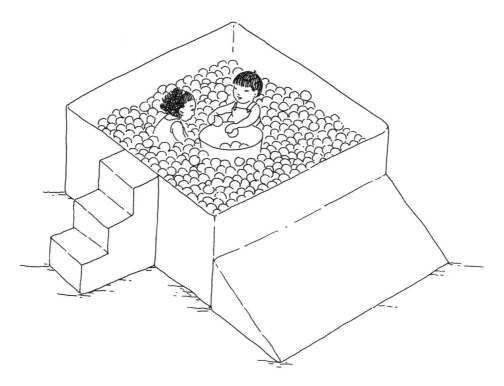

SENSORY MOTOR
Activity 9: Ball Pool

Set up equipment for the children to use to get into and out of an enclosure or "pool" of balls. For example, the children could climb over a series of bolsters or walk up steps. Encourage the children to "follow the path" and get into the pool by sliding in or jumping in feet-first. Once a child is in the pool, encourage him to explore the sensation of being suspended by the balls. Some play possibilities include pretending to swim, searching for stuffed animals hidden under the balls, collecting balls of a certain color, and throwing balls at a target. If two children are in the pool, encourage them to play together.

OBJECTIVES
- Increase proprioceptive awareness;
- Improve tactile discrimination;
- Enhance motor planning;
- Improve tolerance of an unstable surface;
- Improve ability to move on an unstable surface;
- Improve visual discrimination and figure-ground perception;
- Increase eye-hand coordination; and
- Increase color recognition.

EQUIPMENT/SUPPLIES
- Large enclosure for the balls (commercial-type tubs or pools are the sturdiest)
- Balls about two inches in diameter to fill the pool to a height between the waist and chest of the children
- Equipment to lead into and out of the pool (e.g., bolsters, steps, and ramp)
- Stuffed animals

- Target (e.g., plastic hoop or bucket)
- Floor mats

SUGGESTIONS
- Introduce a fearful child to the pool by having her sit on your lap or a bolster in the pool.
- If a child refuses to get into the pool, entice the child into playing with balls placed inside a shallow enclosure, such as an inner tube on the mat.
- Allow an anxious child to play alone in the pool.
- Set up different ways for the children to enter and exit the pool.
- From session to session, vary the equipment leading into the pool.

Activity 10: Tactile Tunnel

Have the children crawl through the tunnel. Encourage them to touch the various materials and objects placed at intervals along the tunnel.

OBJECTIVES
- Increase tolerance of different textures;
- Increase muscle tone by crawling; and
- Improve motor planning.

EQUIPMENT/SUPPLIES
- Tunnel made of canvas/parachute material measuring four to five feet long
- Material and objects of different textures (e.g., furry blankets or stuffed animals)
- Carpet remnants and fabric pieces

SUGGESTIONS
- Shorten the tunnel for a fearful child.
- Have the parent call out to a hesitant child from the far end of the tunnel.
- Observe for a child's tendency to pull away from or avoid certain textures.
- Increase the difficulty by placing the tunnel on top of pillows or bolsters.
- Include the tunnel as part of an obstacle course.

SENSORY MOTOR
Activity 11: Toy Grab Bag

Show the children two or three familiar toys or objects. Have the children feel them. Together with the children, name the toys/objects. Place them in a cloth or paper bag. Then play the game in one of two ways:

1. Encourage the child to reach into the bag and pull out a toy/object. After the child has pulled it out, ask, "What is it?" If the child does not respond, you name it. Encourage the child to say the name. Pass the bag to the next child to play the game.
2. Name one of the toys/objects and ask the child to find it by reaching into the bag. Discourage peeking. If the child pulls out the wrong thing, encourage her to try again. When the correct toy/object has been found, tell the child to repeat the name. Then, pass the bag to the next child to play the game.

OBJECTIVES
- Enhance tactile discrimination;
- Improve manipulation;
- Expand vocabulary; and
- Improve turn-taking.

EQUIPMENT/SUPPLIES
- Paper or cloth bag
- Various familiar small toys and objects: ball, stuffed animal, squeeze toy, doll, spoon, cup, comb, and sock

SUGGESTIONS
- Simplify the game at first by placing only two objects in the bag. Later, you may increase the number.
- In the beginning, select objects that are dissimilar in shape and texture (e.g., comb and sock). Later, you may choose items that are more similar (e.g., stuffed animal and cloth doll).
- Manually assist a child who is having difficulty grasping and manipulating a toy.

SENSORY MOTOR

Activity 12: "Open, Shut Them" Song With Gloves

Help the children put a glove on each hand. Lead the children in the song as you demonstrate the accompanying motions:

Open, shut them; open, shut them.
(Open and close fists.)
Give a little clap, clap, clap.
(Clap hands.)
Open, shut them; open, shut them.
(Open and close fists.)
Put them in your lap, lap, lap.
(Tap hands on lap.)
Creep them; creep them; creep them.
Right up to your chin, chin, chin.
(Crawl fingers of one hand from abdomen up to chin or up opposite arm to chin.)
Open wide your little mouth
(Pause briefly with mouth open.)
But do not let them in.
(Close mouth after saying "in" and bring fingers up to tap on chin or lower lip.)

Next, instruct the children to place their hands on the table or floor with open palms face down, fingers extended. Press firmly on each finger and count each finger as it is touched. Alternatively, you can pull on each finger as you count.

OBJECTIVES
- Increase sensory awareness of the fingers and hands;
- Improve coordination for grasp and release; and
- Improve tactile discrimination of the fingers.

EQUIPMENT/SUPPLIES
- Small cloth gloves

SUGGESTIONS
- If a child initially refuses to put on the gloves, encourage her to sing the song and learn the motions. Eventually she may wear the gloves.
- Physically assist a child having difficulty performing the hand motions.
- If the child puts the gloves on without assistance, correct placement of each finger in the gloves is not critical for the ''Open, Shut Them'' song.

SENSORY MOTOR
Activity 13: Finding Hidden Toys

Place the tactile medium and objects in the container and mix them so that the objects are distributed throughout and are hidden in the medium. Have the children feel with their hands to find the toys, shapes, or balls. When a child is able to see an object, ask him to name it.

OBJECTIVES
- Decrease tactile defensiveness;
- Improve tactile discrimination; and
- Enhance visual discrimination.

EQUIPMENT/SUPPLIES
- Small toys, plastic shapes, or small balls of different textures
- Tactile medium such as dry rice, macaroni, beans, corn meal, oatmeal, pieces of crumpled paper, or sand
- Container for the tactile medium that allows room for moving around the toys and the tactile medium
- Large plastic or cloth sheet to put under the container

SUGGESTIONS
- Put a large plastic or cloth sheet under the container to aid in clean-up.
- If the container holding the tactile medium is small, have the children take turns searching for the hidden objects.
- For the child who resists new tactile media, hide the objects only halfway and gradually bury them deeper.
- First, hide relatively large objects in a medium having a uniform texture, such as cornmeal. During later sessions, progress to hiding smaller objects in a medium having a less even texture, such as macaroni.

SENSORY MOTOR
Activity 14: Play Dough Fun

Give each child a portion of commercial or "homemade" play dough of one or more colors, a rolling pin or dowel, and some figure or shape cutters. Encourage the children to manipulate the play dough to make small balls, snakes, pancakes, and cutout shapes. Encourage them to name what they are making (e.g., "pizza," "snake," or "dog"). Have them say the color and shape of their cutouts. The children can decorate the cutout figures with different objects, such as beans for eyes and noses and shredded paper for hair. Other possible activities include pinching the dough balls, picking up dough balls and putting them in a container, poking holes in the dough with fingers, and squeezing a ball of dough in the hand.

OBJECTIVES
- Improve tolerance for tactile media;
- Increase proprioceptive awareness of the hands and arms;
- Improve muscle strength in the arms, hands, and fingers;
- Improve gross grasp and fingertip grasp; and
- Learn to name and discriminate shapes and colors.

EQUIPMENT/SUPPLIES
- Commercial or "homemade" play dough (see recipe in Appendix E)
- Wooden dowels or child-size rolling pins
- Figure or shape cutters
- Dried beans, macaroni, or shredded paper

SUGGESTIONS
- Have a reluctant child first use a rolling pin and cutters. Gradually encourage more direct contact with the play dough.
- Change texture of the play dough by adding water, cornmeal, or rice.
- Press a child's hand into the dough to make the child's handprint. Count the fingers as you press them into the dough. Then, help the child count the imprints of the fingers.
- Encourage the children to stand up while they work, in order to apply more force as they manipulate the dough.

SENSORY MOTOR
Activity 15: Building With Blocks

Encourage the child to build a "house" with cardboard blocks. If the child does not begin, demonstrate building a simple three-block tower. Leave your tower up and assist the child as needed in building a similar structure. Then, depending upon the child's interest and skill, encourage her to knock down the house or make it taller. Have the child build another house. Show the child a stuffed animal or car and "hide" it behind the house. Have the child knock down the house to find the toy. Next, show the child how to build a "garage," including a roof. Leave your example up as she builds the garage. Have her park a car in the garage and use a block as a door. Then ask her to open the door to get the car.

OBJECTIVES
- Increase eye-hand coordination;
- Improve perception of spatial relations;
- Increase imitation;
- Enhance constructive ability;
- Increase understanding of means-end and cause-effect relationships; and
- Increase ability to follow simple directions.

EQUIPMENT/SUPPLIES
- Cardboard blocks
- Stuffed animal
- Toy car

SUGGESTIONS
- Use hand-over-hand assistance for a child with poor visual and/or motor skills.
- As the child's skill level increases, have the child build in more complex and creative ways without examples.
- Vary the blocks set out, with respect to color, size, and shape.

SENSORY MOTOR

Activity 16: Blowing Fun

Select and demonstrate one blowing activity with a visual or audible result. Then have the children try the activity. Suggested activities include blowing a small feather off the palm of the hand and blowing cotton balls, cereal loops, or other lightweight, safe objects into the air with a toy pipe. Other possibilities are blowing soap bubbles from a bubble wand, blowing bubbles with a drinking straw in a cup of water, and blowing a toy instrument or whistle.

OBJECTIVES
- Learn how to force air through the mouth;
- Increase lip closure; and
- Improve muscle tone of the lips.

EQUIPMENT/SUPPLIES
- Toy pipes
- Cotton balls or cereal loops
- Bubble solution
- Bubble wands
- Cups of water
- Straws
- Feathers
- Whistles
- Toy horns

SUGGESTIONS
- For a child having difficulty blowing, let her feel your breath blowing a feather off her hand.
- If a child opens her mouth too wide, form her mouth into an "O" with your fingers.
- Demonstrate coughing as an initial way of forcing air out of the mouth.

SENSORY MOTOR
Activity 17: Blowing Like the Wind

Demonstrate how the children can pretend to be the "wind" by blowing through a straw to make things move on a table. Have the children blow a small pile of tissue paper, feathers, or lightweight balls. Also, the children could blow on a puddle of paint on wax paper so that the paint moves out in streams.

OBJECTIVE
- Increase lip closure;
- Improve muscle tone of the lips; and
- Increase ability to sustain blowing.

EQUIPMENT/SUPPLIES
- Plastic straws about four inches long (regular straws cut in half)
- Small pieces of paper
- Lightweight balls, such as table tennis balls
- Small feathers
- Thinned paint (tempra or acrylic)
- Wax paper

SUGGESTIONS
- For a child who can't blow through a straw, first have him practice blowing without a straw or blowing bubbles from a wand.
- If a child does not seal his lips around the straw, use your fingers to assist in lip closure.
- Have a more skillful child blow a ball through a cardboard goal or tunnel.

SENSORY MOTOR
Activity 18: Tongue Gymnastics

Demonstrate licking the upper lip. Ask the child to imitate you. After his first attempt, using a spoon or tongue depressor, place a small amount of food (from his plate) on the child's upper lip. Again demonstrate licking off your upper lip as you ask him to lick off his lip. Repeat this process with the bottom lip and sides of the lips. Demonstrate sticking out your tongue and ask the child to copy you. Then hold the spoon or tongue depressor in front of the child's mouth. Ask him to lick it. Then ask him to open his mouth so that you can place a small amount of food between his cheeks and gums using the spoon or depressor. Direct him to touch his tongue to that area. Repeat, putting the food in different areas between his cheeks and gums.

OBJECTIVES
- Enhance sensory awareness of mouth structures;
- Improve volitional tongue movements;
- Improve ability to imitate tongue movements; and
- Increase tolerance for different tastes and smells.

EQUIPMENT/SUPPLIES
- Spreadable food (e.g., peanut butter, pudding, jelly, or yogurt)
- Serving spoon
- Paper plates
- Individual spoons or tongue depressors
- Plastic or latex gloves

SUGGESTIONS
- Do not use peanut butter with a child having swallowing difficulties.
- Use the spoon to tap the area you wish the child to lick.
- When food is placed inside the mouth, tap on the outside of the face over the area where you wish the child to move his tongue.
- For a child having difficulty imitating the movements, instruct him to watch you and then watch himself in a tabletop mirror.
- Place small pieces of soft food between the cheeks and gums of a child who can chew.
- Use plastic gloves if a child is allergic to latex.

Activity 19: Tasting Party

Dip a cotton swab or toothbrush into a flavored liquid or puree. Encourage the child first to smell the swab and then taste the flavor on the swab. Encourage the child to move the brush or swab around to different areas of the lips and mouth. Then give the child a drink of water. Repeat the procedure again with a new swab or rinsed toothbrush dipped into a different flavor.

OBJECTIVE
- Enhance taste and smell discrimination; and
- Increase awareness of mouth structures.

EQUIPMENT/SUPPLIES
- Juices (sweet and sour), flavors, extracts, lemon glycerin swabs, fruit purees or sauces
- Cotton swabs or toothbrushes
- Cups and water

SUGGESTIONS
- Dilute strong flavors with water. Dilute flavors even more for a child resistant to tasting.
- Give the end of a dipped gauze strip to a child having difficulty getting a swab or toothbrush into the mouth.
- Playfully touch the toothbrush or swab to a reluctant child's lips. Try gradually to get it into the child's mouth.

SENSORY MOTOR
Activity 20: Smelling Party

Prior to this session, place a small amount of the dry spices into film containers. Place a few drops of the liquids on separate cotton gauze pads and then place the pads into additional film containers. Label the tops of the containers. At the time of the activity, open one container. Have each child smell the fragrance. Ask the children what it smells like. Suggest appropriate foods such as "cookies" for cinnamon or "spaghetti" for garlic. Also, you may make sounds such as "mmm" for some smells or "phew" for others. After closing the first container, open another one and continue.

OBJECTIVES
- Increase awareness of smells;
- Decrease sensitivity associated with the smell of different foods; and
- Improve verbalization about smells and the association of smells with foods.

EQUIPMENT/SUPPLIES
- Small plastic film containers with lids
- Variety of aromatic spices and flavorings such as lemon, orange, and vanilla extracts, broken cinnamon sticks, whole cloves, curry powder, and minced dried garlic or onions
- Gauze pads
- Container in which to store film containers
- Permanent marker to label the film containers
- Alcohol wipes

SUGGESTIONS
- Alternate pleasant or less potent smells such as cinnamon or cloves with more potent smells such as onions, garlic, or lemon.
- Use caution when introducing smells. Some children gag at certain smells. If a particular smell triggers a gag response in a child, do not present that smell again to that child for a few months.
- Wave an open container several times under the nose of a child who does not seem to "sniff-in" the smell. The child most likely will get a bit of the smell just by breathing.
- Do not touch the container to the child's face. If the container touches the child's face, wipe the container with an alcohol wipe and let it dry before covering it again.

COGNITIVE/LANGUAGE

Activity 21: "Where is _____?" Song

The children and staff sit in a circle. Select one child to identify first; for example, the child sitting to the left of the leader. Sing these words to the tune of "Frere Jacques:"

Where is (child's name)?
Where is (child's name)?

Pause and wait for the child to respond in some way (e.g., by vocalizing or raising a hand). A staff member may need to prompt the child. When the child has given some response to his name, allow him to see himself in the mirror. Then, complete the song by instructing everyone to sing:

Here I am. Here I am.
How are you today? How are you today?
I am fine. I am fine.

OBJECTIVES
- Increase awareness of separate identity;
- Improve orientation to one's name;
- Develop listening skills;
- Improve attention span; and
- Increase turn-taking ability.

EQUIPMENT/SUPPLIES
- One large hand mirror

SUGGESTIONS
- Repeat the song until each child's name has been called.
- If the children quickly learn to recognize their own names, randomly use their names in the song to increase the attention demands of the activity.

COGNITIVE/LANGUAGE
Activity 22: Feather Touch

Give each child a feather. As you name a particular body part, have all the children simultaneously touch that particular body part (e.g., head, nose, or arm) with their feather. Alternatively, ask each child, in turn, to touch a certain part of his or her body.

OBJECTIVES
- Increase awareness of the body parts;
- Increase recognition of names of body parts;
- Improve ability to point to the body parts; and
- Develop listening skills.

EQUIPMENT/SUPPLIES
- Feather for each child

SUGGESTIONS
- If a child needs visual cues, point to the body part on yourself or show a picture of the body part as you say the name of the body part.
- For variety, give each child other tactile items, such as a piece of fur, a soft foam ball, or cotton ball, to use.
- Have each child touch a particular part of your body as you name it.

COGNITIVE/LANGUAGE

Activity 23: Animal Names and Sounds

Have the child take a toy animal out of a container. Ask "What is this?" Name the animal if the child does not do so. Encourage the child to imitate saying the animal's name. Ask "What does the (animal's name) say?" Tell the child the sound if he does not respond appropriately. Encourage imitation of the animal sound. Then have the same child or a different child (if this is a group activity) select another animal figure. Repeat the same steps.

OBJECTIVES

- Improve association of names and sounds with particular animals;
- Increase imitation;
- Enhance prompted use of sounds and words; and
- Increase understanding of simple questions.

EQUIPMENT/SUPPLIES

- Toy animals: dog, cat, cow, sheep, and duck
- Container for animal figures

SUGGESTIONS

- Have a child with limited verbal skills watch your face as you carefully enunciate the word or sound.
- Reinforce any attempts at saying the animal name or sound.
- If English is not the child's first language, be aware that the child may have learned different animal sounds.
- Use pictures of animals to elicit naming and sound-making.

Activity 24: Matching Picture and Object

Point to each of two or three pictures of familiar objects. Talk briefly about each picture. Then present the corresponding objects. Ask a child to point to a particular object corresponding to one picture. Encourage the child to talk about the object and picture by asking him simple questions. Repeat this process with another child.

OBJECTIVES
- Increase the ability to identify familiar objects and pictures of them upon request;
- Improve the ability to follow simple directions;
- Increase the imitation of sounds and words; and
- Increase verbal responses to questions.

EQUIPMENT/SUPPLIES
- Picture books/cards and corresponding objects. For example, a spoon and a picture of a spoon

SUGGESTIONS
- If the child's attention or memory is brief, present one picture and its corresponding object at a time.
- Name the pictures and objects several times.
- If the child can make only word approximations or signs, reinforce those efforts.
- Choose pictures and objects with the same theme, such as food, clothing, or animals.
- Reverse the process. Present the objects first and have the child identify the corresponding pictures.

COGNITIVE/LANGUAGE
Activity 25: "Stop" and "Go" Game

When a child is riding on a piece of equipment that can be easily and quickly stopped, introduce the child to the idea of starting and stopping the motion on verbal commands. Begin by saying, "go!" and then start propelling the equipment. After a moment or so, say, "stop!" and stop the motion of the equipment. Next, have the child give you the verbal commands of "go!" and "stop!" and you follow her directions appropriately.

OBJECTIVES
- Improve auditory attention and processing; and
- Increase understanding and the use of verbal commands.

EQUIPMENT/SUPPLIES
- Equipment such as a merry-go-round, rocking toy, or swing

SUGGESTIONS
- Reinforce word approximations (and signs if the child has no verbalizations).
- Provide a greater challenge by having the child say, "One, two, three, go!" before you begin the motion of the equipment.
- Have the child start and stop an action, such as jumping on a trampoline, upon her own or your verbal commands.

COGNITIVE/LANGUAGE
Activity 26: Forgotten Rhyme

Lead the children in reciting a well-known nursery rhyme such as "Patty Cake, Patty Cake." Show appropriate picture(s) to illustrate the rhyme. When the children are familiar with the rhyme, again lead a recitation of it. Pause periodically before key words as if you have forgotten the next word. Encourage the children to fill in the missing word. Use the picture(s) to cue the missing word. Then resume reciting the rhyme.

OBJECTIVES
- Increase auditory attention and memory;
- Improve the association of words and pictures;
- Increase expressive vocabulary; and
- Improve visual attention.

EQUIPMENT/SUPPLIES
- Picture(s) to illustrate each rhyme

SUGGESTIONS
- Reinforce word and sign approximations.
- Use a familiar song, such as "Wheels on the Bus," or "Twinkle, Twinkle, Little Star."

COGNITIVE/LANGUAGE

Activity 27: Action Songs

The children and staff form a circle. With musical accompaniment, sing action songs, such as "Head, Shoulder, Knees, and Toes," "Eensy, Weensy Spider," "Hokey Pokey," and "Ring Around The Rosie." Model appropriate movements for the children. Assist children who cannot perform the actions independently.

OBJECTIVES

- Improve listening skills;
- Increase the ability to follow simple directions;
- Improve the ability to imitate actions;
- Improve the ability to move rhythmically; and
- Increase verbalization.

EQUIPMENT/SUPPLIES

- Cassette tape player or record player
- Tapes or records of action songs

SUGGESTIONS

- First practice a song and its actions without the musical recording so that you can set the pace.
- Allow a child to choose one of two songs for the group to perform.
- Have a child who is adept at a song and its actions stand in the center of the group and lead the song.

COGNITIVE/LANGUAGE
Activity 28: Words for Play

Select four to six words for particular emphasis during the Gross Motor/Language Center. They could include some from the monthly concepts, such as *up/down* or *yellow*. Other words relevant to play also could be chosen, for instance *more/done* or *stop/go*. Post the words so the staff and parents have a visual reminder. As the children play on the equipment and appropriate situations arise, emphasize the words that correspond to the equipment or actions. For example, state that the slide is yellow and that the child is climbing up the steps. Keep your language simple, just stating the words alone. Encourage the children to imitate these words.

OBJECTIVES
- Increase the understanding of concepts related to color, shape, spatial relationships and movement;
- Improve receptive language; and
- Increase expressive language.

EQUIPMENT/SUPPLIES
- Equipment that reflects monthly concepts and/or relevant words

SUGGESTIONS
- Reinforce word approximations by imitating and expanding upon them.
- For a child with very limited expressive language and limited attention, select one word or a word pair (e.g., *on/off*) on which to work.
- For a child with greater language skills, include the words in a phrase or simple sentence, such as "climbing *on*," or "go *down*."

COGNITIVE/LANGUAGE
Activity 29: Shell Game

While the child is watching, name and then hide a toy under one of the two or three small containers. Ask the child to find the toy, then name it. If this is a one-on-one activity, repeat the game as long as she is interested. If this is a group activity, repeat the game with the next child.

OBJECTIVES

- Improve visual attention and memory;
- Increase awareness of object permanence;
- Improve the ability to point to and name familiar objects;
- Increase responsiveness to simple questions; and
- Improve the ability to follow verbal directions.

EQUIPMENT/SUPPLIES

- Small containers (e.g., cups, boxes, or bowls)
- Small toys

SUGGESTIONS

- Use a sound-making toy, such as a squeaky toy, to maintain a child's attention until you hide the toy.
- Encourage continued attention by pointing to each container as you ask, "Is the (toy's name) here?"
- Change the toy being hidden, in order to sustain the child's interest.
- Increase the difficulty by adding another container or toy.

COGNITIVE/LANGUAGE
Activity 30: Big and Little Boxes

Let the children see the big box. Have them crawl in and explore it. Show the children the little box and let them hold it. Talk about how one box is big and the child can crawl inside it and how the other box is little and the child cannot crawl into it. Encourage the children to say "big" and "little." Have the children point to the appropriate box as you say "big" or "little."

OBJECTIVES
- Increase understanding of the concepts of big and little;
- Improve the ability to follow simple directions; and
- Increase verbalization.

EQUIPMENT/SUPPLIES
- Large cardboard box (appliance size)
- Small cardboard box (hand size)

SUGGESTIONS
- Talk about how the child cannot hold the big box in his hand but can hold the little box.
- Have the children experience the size difference between other objects, such as a gym ball and hand-size ball or an adult-size chair and child-size chair.

COGNITIVE/LANGUAGE

Activity 31: Touching Hot and Cold

Pass the hot-water bottle around. Encourage the children to touch the bottle lightly. Ask them how it feels. Have each child attempt to say "hot." Ask: "What do we eat or drink that is hot?" Repeat appropriate responses (e.g., if a child says "soup," you can respond, "soup is hot"). Next, pass the bowl of ice cubes around. Ask how it feels. Have each child attempt to say "cold." Ask: "What do we eat or drink that is cold?" Again, reinforce appropriate answers.

OBJECTIVES

- Increase understanding of the concepts of *hot* and *cold;*
- Improve verbal responsiveness to questions; and
- Increase expressive vocabulary.

EQUIPMENT/SUPPLIES

- Hot-water bottle filled with warm water or a microwaveable heat pack
- Bowl of ice cubes or a "blue ice" freezer pack

SUGGESTIONS

- Make sure the items are not too hot or too cold for skin contact.
- Have tasting experiences of hot and cold foods, such as soup and Popsicles, at snack time.
- Talk about hot and cold weather.
- Show pictures of clothing appropriate for hot and for cold weather.

COGNITIVE/LANGUAGE
Activity 32: Circle Grab Bag

Place circular objects in the grab bag. Have one child at a time pull one item out of the bag. Help each child identify the object. Have him feel and trace around the object with his hand. Emphasize that each object has a circular shape. Conclude the activity by having each child use a finger to trace a circle in the damp sand. If necessary, physically guide the child's hand as she draws the circle.

OBJECTIVES
- Improve understanding of the concept of circle;
- Increase visual and tactile-kinesthetic recognition of the circular shape of objects;
- Increase the ability to follow a simple direction; and
- Improve turn-taking ability.

EQUIPMENT/SUPPLIES
- Assorted circular-shaped objects of various sizes and colors (e.g., lids, toy plates, puzzle pieces, or buttons)
- Grab bag
- Tray of damp sand

SUGGESTIONS
- Mix other shapes into the grab bag and have each child pull out one that feels like a circle.
- Introduce the triangle and square shapes by this same method.

COGNITIVE/LANGUAGE

Activity 33: Brown Bear, Brown Bear *Story*

Read the book "Brown Bear, Brown Bear, What do You See?" slowly once. Allow time for any language expression from the children. Then go through the story again, emphasizing the color of each animal. Talk about the animals and the sounds they make. Encourage the children to repeat the colors, animal names, and animal sounds. Ask the children to point to the colors and animals as you name them.

OBJECTIVES
- Increase recognition and the naming of colors and animals;
- Improve expressive language;
- Increase attention span;
- Increase auditory memory and listening skills; and
- Develop positive feelings toward books.

EQUIPMENT/SUPPLIES
- Book: *Brown Bear, Brown Bear, What do You See?*, by Bill Martin, Jr.

SUGGESTIONS
- Show enthusiasm and use pauses for effect as you read.
- Reinforce any attempts at verbalization or signing.
- Have the children match colored blocks to the colors or toy figures to the animals in the story.

COGNITIVE/LANGUAGE

Activity 34: Sharing Toys From Home

When the children are gathered in a circle, hold up one toy and ask, "Who brought this toy?" The child should be encouraged to respond by saying "me," his name, or by raising his hand. Next, you or the child (if he is able) names the toy and describes it according to the monthly concept (for example, *brown dog*). After the toy has been described, ask the child to come to the front of the circle, retrieve the toy, and return to this seat. Then, ask the child to hold the toy up to show to his peers. If applicable, ask the child to demonstrate how the toy works. Then hold up a different toy and continue as before.

OBJECTIVES

- Improve visual attention and memory;
- Improve self-identification;
- Improve listening skills;
- Increase the ability to follow simple commands; and
- Improve turn-taking.

EQUIPMENT/SUPPLIES

- Container (e.g., plastic laundry basket or large, decorative box)
- Toys brought from home by the children

SUGGESTIONS

- Encourage parents to assist their children in choosing a toy that corresponds with a monthly concept, such as the color or shape.

COGNITIVE/LANGUAGE
Activity 35: Feeding a Baby Doll

While the child watches, pretend to feed a doll with a spoon and plate. Ask the child to do the same. Next, pretend to give the doll a drink from a cup or a bottle. Ask the child to imitate you. Give the child verbal and physical cues/assistance as needed.

OBJECTIVES
- Increase understanding of simple instructions;
- Improve the ability to follow simple directions; and
- Increase imitation of actions.

EQUIPMENT/SUPPLIES
- Doll
- Cup
- Bottle
- Plate
- Spoon

SUGGESTIONS
- If the child is uninterested in the doll, you could substitute a stuffed animal.
- Demonstrate how to comb the doll's hair and ask the child to imitate that action.
- Point to the doll's body parts as you name them. Then ask the child to point to particular body parts.
- Once the child can successfully imitate these actions, try giving the verbal commands without any demonstration.

Activity 36: Tactile Pool

Put an inch or two of a tactile medium into a plastic wading pool with a large plastic sheet or cloth underneath. Place utensils for scooping, pouring, and holding the medium. Also, provide toys or objects that can be hidden in the medium. Encourage two to three children to play in the pool. If the children are willing, have them step into the pool with their bare feet. Promote the sharing of toys, taking of turns, and interactive play. For example, one child could hold a bucket while another fills it. Another example would be having one child hide a toy in the medium and another child hunt for the toy. Encourage conversation by asking the children about what they are doing.

OBJECTIVES

- Increase toy-sharing and turn-taking;
- Enhance interactive and pretend play;
- Decrease tactile defensiveness;
- Develop body percept related to the feet;
- Increase expressive language; and
- Improve eye-hand coordination and fine motor control.

EQUIPMENT/SUPPLIES

- Plastic wading pool
- Large plastic or cloth sheet
- Tactile medium, such as sand, cornmeal, uncooked rice or beans, or crumpled paper (enough to fill enclosure or pool one to two inches deep)
- Buckets, cups, spoons, shovels, scoops, rakes, and sand wheels
- Toys to hide, such as small figures, shapes, balls, etc.

SUGGESTIONS

- If a child resists getting into the pool, encourage her to squat or kneel alongside the pool and place her hands into the pool. Later, try placing a small amount of the tactile medium on her feet.
- Allow a child who is "working through" an aversion to the medium to play in the pool alone at first.
- Suggest an imaginary scenario, such as playing at the beach or digging for buried treasure.

SOCIALIZATION/ORGANIZATION OF BEHAVIOR
Activity 37: Telephone Buddies

Sit in a quiet area with a child. As you hold the receiver of one toy telephone, make the sound of a telephone ringing. Encourage the child to pick up the other receiver. Say, "Hello." Encourage the child to answer "Hello." Continue the conversation with common questions such as "How are you?" or "What are you doing?" Wait for the child to respond. If the child does not respond, suggest appropriate responses such as "fine" or "playing." After a few minutes of conversation, say, "Bye-bye." Wait for the child to reply, "Bye-bye." Then both of you should hang up the receivers.

OBJECTIVES
- Increase pretend play of familiar activities;
- Increase social interaction;
- Improve imitation of words and activities; and
- Enhance turn-taking in conversation.

EQUIPMENT/SUPPLIES
- Two play telephones

SUGGESTIONS
- Speak slowly and simply.
- Have the child begin the call and lead the conversation.
- Assist two children in conversing on the telephones.

SOCIALIZATION/ORGANIZATION OF BEHAVIOR
Activity 38: Ball Play in Pairs

Pair up children to play ball together. Select one of three types of ball play: rolling/catching, throwing at a target, or kicking. For rolling/catching, have the two children sit on the floor facing each other with their legs spread apart. Have the children roll the ball on the floor to each other. Encourage one child to cue the other by calling out the other child's name or a simple word like "ball" just before passing the ball. For throwing at a target, have the children take turns at throwing. When it is each child's turn, say "(child's name)'s turn!" Kicking can be done from one child to another or toward a target. Kicking from one to another can be structured like rolling/catching, and kicking toward a target can be carried out like throwing at a target.

OBJECTIVES
- Improve turn-taking;
- Increase social interaction;
- Improve name recognition;
- Increase visual and auditory attention;
- Improve eye-hand and eye-foot coordination;
- Enhance motor planning; and
- Develop equilibrium reactions.

EQUIPMENT/SUPPLIES
- Balls of various textures, colors, and sizes
- Targets, such as an inner tube, box, laundry basket, or foam blocks

SUGGESTIONS
- Some pairs of children may require the assistance of two adults.
- Make the targets large enough and the distance between child-to-target and child-to-child short enough so that the children can be successful. Increase the difficulty as the children's skills improve.
- Have each child choose a ball. First use one ball and then switch to using the other one.

SOCIALIZATION/ORGANIZATION OF BEHAVIOR
Activity 39: Dollhouse Play

Encourage the child to place the furniture in appropriate rooms of the dollhouse. Then encourage the child to place a figure on the furniture, such as laying the figure to sleep on the bed. Encourage the child to name the room, furniture, and activity. If the child cannot say what the figure is doing, you can describe it in simple terms such as "Time to sleep" or "Girl go night-night." Continue the activity by having the child play with the furniture and figures in other rooms of the dollhouse.

OBJECTIVES
- Increase pretend play of familiar activities;
- Enhance knowledge of the names for rooms of a house;
- Increase awareness of the locations for everyday activities, such as sleeping, bathing, and eating;
- Improve fine motor coordination;
- Increase verbalization; and
- Improve praxis in relation to everyday activities.

EQUIPMENT/SUPPLIES
- Toy house
- Durable toy furniture
- Dolls or other figures

SUGGESTIONS
- Give a child with limited initiative or environmental awareness more verbal and physical prompting.
- Have the child use the figure to act out part of her daily routine.
- Have two children engage in this activity together.

Activity 40: Pretend Play Centers

Prepare a play center with appropriate items according to the selected theme. Sample settings include "house," "store," or "restaurant." Encourage two to three children to enter the play area. Depending on the children's developmental levels, facilitate simple play, such as pretending to wash dishes, or a more complex scenario, such as taking orders at a restaurant, serving the food, and accepting payment for the bill. You may need to model an action, such as feeding a doll, then ask the child to imitate that action. Also, encourage interaction by asking one child to help another one, suggesting different roles for the children to play, and coaching them as needed. However, do have them make choices about what to buy at the "store" or what food to order. Promote receptive and expressive language by naming objects and actions, asking questions, and expanding on what the children say.

OBJECTIVES
- Increase imitation;
- Enhance creativity;
- Enhance pretend play;
- Increase interactive play;
- Develop sequencing ability;
- Enhance receptive and expressive language;
- Increase ability to make choices;
- Increase visual discrimination;
- Improve fine motor skills; and
- Improve self-care skills.

EQUIPMENT/SUPPLIES
- Items to define the play center area, such as room dividers, a play house, a play kitchen, a table, chairs, and shelves
- Props appropriate to the theme
- **Store:** A shopping cart, a cash register, shopping bags, empty food boxes, plastic food, and cans

Restaurant: Play dishes, play food, a cash register, a note pad, and a pencil

House: A table, chairs, dishes, food, dolls, doll clothes, a kitchen center, a broom, and a vacuum cleaner

Hair salon: Dolls, doll chairs, combs, brushes, foam soap, and water

SUGGESTIONS

- Have the same play center set up for a few sessions so that the children can become familiar with it, increasing their willingness and ability to participate.
- Include a child with limited pretend-play skills by having him be the recipient of another child's actions, such as having "lunch" served to him. Assist the child, using verbal and physical cues, to respond appropriately.
- Have enough items to entice the children into creative play, but not so many items that they have difficulty staying focused.
- When setting up a playhouse, vary the type of domestic activity (e.g., cooking, dish washing, housecleaning, and child care) from time to time.
- Encourage a child to perform a series of actions by cueing, "First, we _____." "Now what do we do?" and "Next, we _____."

SOCIALIZATION/ORGANIZATION OF BEHAVIOR
Activity 41: Nesting Cups

Draw a child's attention to a set of nesting cups on the table. Observe how the child first plays with the cups. Encourage his play and use language to describe his actions and concepts relative to the cups. For example, if the child builds a tower, you and the child might say: "big," "little," "tall," or "fall down." After a few minutes, suggest that the child play with the cups in other ways. If the child does not seem to have an idea, show him another way, such as matching the cups by color or using them as containers for small toys.

OBJECTIVES
- Enhance creative play;
- Improve visual discrimination of size and color;
- Increase eye-hand coordination and dexterity; and
- Expand receptive and expressive vocabulary for size, color, and spatial concepts.

EQUIPMENT/SUPPLIES
- Nesting cups
- Small figures or other toys to use with cups

SUGGESTIONS
- Make size discrimination easier by taking away some of the intermediate sizes.
- Make color discrimination easier by using only two colors of cups.
- On another day, introduce yet another way of playing with the cups.
- Do this activity with nesting boxes and blocks or other versatile toys.

SOCIALIZATION/ORGANIZATION OF BEHAVIOR
Activity 42: Transition Songs

"Here We Are Together"

Sing when the children are first gathered in a circle. Sing these words to the tune of "In and Out the Windows:"

Here we are together, together, together.
Here we are together, together right now.
Here's (child's name) *and* (child's name) *and . . .*

Continue until each child has been named, and end it by singing:

Here we are together, together right now.

Toy Pick-up Song

Sing as the staff and children put away the toys used during the Exploratory Play period. Sing these words to the tune of "Here We Go 'Round the Mulberry Bush:"

It's time to put the toys away,
The toys away, the toys away.
It's time to put the toys away,
So we can go to centers.

"Good-bye Song"

Sing at the children's departure time. Sing these words to the tune of "Goodnight Ladies:"

Good-bye (child's name)
Good-bye (child's name)
Good-bye (child's name)
It's time to say good-bye.

Repeat until all the children have been named in the song, then use "everyone" if you need another name to complete the song.

OBJECTIVES

- Improve name recognition for self and peers;
- Enhance the ability to transition from one activity to another;
- Increase the willingness and ability to put toys away; and
- Increase expressive language.

EQUIPMENT/SUPPLIES

- None

SUGGESTIONS

- Sing these songs during every program session so that the children recognize them as transition signals.
- While singing "Here We Are Together," have the children hold hands and sway side to side.
- Wave good-bye to each child when named and encourage the child to return the wave.

SOCIALIZATION/ORGANIZATION OF BEHAVIOR
Activity 43: "All Done" at Snack Time

During Snack Time, encourage a child to remain in his seat until he has completed his snack. If he wanders away from his seat, guide him back. If it is obvious that he has not finished eating and drinking, indicate that he is to finish by stating, "Not done" or "Eat more, please." If you are not certain whether the child wants to eat or drink more, ask "All done?" If the child responds affirmatively (verbally, if possible), state, "Wait." Hold the basin near the child. Direct the child to "put dishes away" or "clean up" by placing his cup, bowl, and napkin in the basin. After the child has completed this task, indicate that the child may leave the table by your saying, "All done." Encourage him to say the phrase.

OBJECTIVES
- Enhance the ability to complete one task before beginning another;
- Increase the understanding and use of words as signals;
- Improve the ability to wait briefly; and
- Improve the ability to anticipate the next event.

EQUIPMENT/SUPPLIES
- Usual set-up for Snack Time

SUGGESTIONS
- Stay near a child who tends to wander, or have the child sit in a chair with an attached tray.
- Encourage the child to express verbally his requests and readiness.

Activity 44: Scooping and Pouring Play

Place the plastic pool on the floor on top of a blanket or large, plastic sheet. Dump the rice or other substance into the pool. Put the utensils and containers on top of the tactile medium. Encourage the children to stand or sit in the pool. Show the children how to use the spoons to fill the containers and pour from one container to another. Promote conversation about what you and they are doing.

OBJECTIVES

- Enhance praxis related to self-feeding skills;
- Improve the skill for scooping with a spoon and pouring liquids;
- Decrease tactile defensiveness;
- Develop body percept related to the feet;
- Increase peer interaction and sharing; and
- Improve receptive and expressive language.

EQUIPMENT/SUPPLIES

- A plastic wading pool
- Plastic spoons and shovels of different sizes and shapes
- Small buckets or plastic bowls
- Plastic glasses or cups
- Tactile medium, such as sand, cornmeal, or uncooked rice or beans (enough to fill enclosure or pool one to two inches deep)
- Blanket, sheet, or ground cover

SUGGESTIONS

- Place the sheet under the pool to facilitate cleanup.
- The tactile media can be stored in plastic bags placed in wash basins.
- Closely supervise the children to prevent eating or throwing of the tactile medium.
- Use hand-over-hand assistance to guide a child having difficulty pouring and scooping.
- Hide small toys in the tactile medium (rice, beans, etc.) and have the children scoop the medium into a bucket as they dig for the "buried treasure" with spoons or shovels.
- For a "hands-only" activity, the tactile medium may be placed in a basin.

Activity 45: Spoon Feeding

Have the child sit in a chair that promotes good sitting posture, including spine and head alignment, knee flexion, and foot support (by the floor or a box). Sit next to the child. Have the child grasp the spoon. With your hand over his, guide him in scooping the food in the dish, bringing the spoon to his mouth, and putting it into his mouth. As his skill increases, reduce your physical assistance by just guiding him from his elbow or providing assistance for only a portion of the sequence, such as when he is scooping the food or inserting the spoon into his mouth.

OBJECTIVES
- Improve optimal body posture for spoon feeding;
- Increase eye-hand coordination and fine motor control;
- Improve oral motor skills; and
- Increase independence.

EQUIPMENT/SUPPLIES
- Spoons of various shapes and sizes
- Bowl or plate with rim
- "Spoon food" (e.g., applesauce or yogurt)
- Paper towels or napkins
- Bib

SUGGESTIONS
- Initially use a thick, sticky food, such as yogurt, pudding, or oatmeal.
- If a child is resistant to trying independent spoon feeding, encourage him to alternate feeding himself with your feeding him.
- Observe whether the child's tongue is flat or curled when the spoon is inserted. If the tongue is curled, use your hand over the child's hand to apply downward pressure with the spoon on the front half of the tongue.
- As a child's skills increase, offer more difficult food to scoop, such as pieces of canned fruit, or canned vegetables, or cereal with milk.

SELF-CARE
Activity 46: Chewing and Biting

Have the child sit in a chair that promotes good sitting posture, including spine and head alignment, knee flexion, and foot support (by the floor or a box). Sit next to or in front of the child. Place a small amount of food between the child's molars. If the child does not begin to chew, use your hand to gently move his jaw up, down, and laterally as you ask him to chew. Once the child has swallowed the food, he may have a small drink. Then place a small amount of food between the molars on the other side of his mouth. When the child has successfully chewed up several small pieces of food without assistance, progress to slightly larger pieces of food. As the child's chewing skills improve, ask him to bite off a piece of cracker after you have placed it between his teeth at the front or side of his mouth. You may need to move his jaw upward until the child learns how to bite with enough pressure. Even after the child can chew and bite independently, you may still need to monitor the quantity of food the child is inserting into his mouth.

OBJECTIVES
- Improve optimal body posture for chewing and biting;
- Increase tactile-kinesthetic awareness of tongue, gums, and cheeks;
- Improve tolerance for different textures and smells;
- Increase oral motor skills; and
- Increase independence.

EQUIPMENT/SUPPLIES
- Soft, crushable foods (e.g., graham crackers, bananas, small pieces of softened cheese, or dry cereal)
- Plate or bowl
- Bib
- Paper towels or napkins
- Cup of water or other drink
- Plastic or latex gloves

SUGGESTIONS

- Begin with a graham cracker, as it is easiest for a child to dissolve and form into a lump for swallowing.
- If a child seems resistant to the texture of the food, encourage exposure to thickened and lumpy foods at Snack Time and at home. Also try the Tasting Party (see Activity 19) with him.
- Have a child experiencing difficulties with tongue movements perform the Tongue Gymnastics and Tasting Party (see Activities 18, 19).
- As the child's skills improve, introduce foods with a long, thin shape (e.g., pretzel sticks or graham cracker strips) and less dissolvability (e.g., dried fruit pieces and cooked vegetables).
- Use plastic gloves if a child is allergic to latex.

Activity 47: Cup Drinking

Have the child sit in a chair that promotes good sitting posture, including spine and head alignment, knee flexion, and foot support (by the floor or a box). Sit next to or in front of the child. Provide hand-over-hand assistance as the child picks up the cup and brings it to his mouth. If the child fails to seal his bottom lip to the cup rim, apply gentle, upward pressure underneath the child's bottom lip with your index finger. Encourage the child to remove the cup from his mouth after each mouthful so that you can check for adequate swallowing. During extended pauses, have the child place the cup on the table. As the child's skills improve, provide less physical and verbal assistance/cueing.

OBJECTIVES
- Improve optimal body posture for cup drinking;
- Increase eye-hand coordination and fine motor control for handling cup;
- Improve oral motor skills; and
- Increase independence.

EQUIPMENT/SUPPLIES
- Various cups (e.g., cups with and without spouts, cups with and without lids, cups with and without handles, and clear cups)
- Bib
- Juice or other drink
- Paper towels or napkins
- Plastic or latex gloves

SUGGESTIONS

- Introduce cup drinking via a cup without a spout. If this proves unsuccessful, then try a cup with a spout.
- If a child has difficulty controlling liquid in the mouth, use thicker liquids (e.g., juice with applesauce or fruit puree added, fruit nectar, milk shake, or yogurt drink).
- If a child moves his jaw up and down as he drinks, apply gentle, upward pressure under his jaw just behind his chin with your middle or index finger.
- Use a cup with a textured surface for a child having difficulty maintaining her grasp of the cup.
- Provide the children with the experience of using uncovered cups.
- Use plastic gloves if a child is allergic to latex.

Activity 48: Straw Drinking

Have the child sit in a chair that promotes good sitting posture, including spine and head alignment, knee flexion, and foot support (by the floor or a box). Sit next to or in front of the child. Dip a plastic straw cut to a length of three to four inches into a small cup of juice. Place your finger over the top of the straw to trap some of the juice in the straw. Put the bottom end of the straw in the child's mouth. As you remove your finger from the top end of the straw, the juice will flow into the child's mouth. Encourage the child to seal her lips around the straw and suck the liquid. If necessary, use your fingers to close the child's lips around the straw. As the child learns to suck more strongly, lower the straw. Next, have the child suck from the straw placed in a small cup held by you or the child. Gradually increase the length of the straw used.

OBJECTIVES

- Improve optimal body posture for straw drinking;
- Improve oral motor skills;
- Increase eye-hand coordination and fine motor control; and
- Increase independence.

EQUIPMENT/SUPPLIES

- Plastic straws of different lengths
- Cups of different sizes
- Juice or other drink
- Bib
- Paper towels or napkins
- Plastic or latex gloves

SUGGESTIONS

- You also can use a juice box or a squeeze bottle made from a honey bear bottle or soft ketchup bottle with aquarium tubing or a flexible straw inserted. Gently squeeze the juice into the child's mouth.
- Encourage greater use of the lips by reducing the length of the straw entering the child's mouth (e.g., place a large bead or a cork with a hole drilled into it, close to the straw end that enters the child's mouth).
- Offer thicker liquids (e.g., milk shake or yogurt drink) to strengthen the child's lips and cheeks.
- Use plastic gloves if a child is allergic to latex.

Activity 49: Paper Doll Dressing

Have the child place a piece of the paper clothing on the doll. Use appropriate cues and questions, such as "Put this shirt on the doll," or "Where does this go?" You may need to demonstrate or guide placement of the clothing. Ask the child to name the clothing placed on the doll. If the child does not say the name, state the name and encourage the child to imitate the word. Reinforce any naming attempt that approximates the desired word, including just the beginning sound or a sign for the clothing. Pass the doll to the next child to place either the same or a different piece of clothing.

OBJECTIVES
- Enhance body percept;
- Heighten awareness of the location on the body for different pieces of clothing;
- Increase recognition and use of names for common pieces of clothing; and
- Increase verbalization.

EQUIPMENT/SUPPLIES
- Cardboard figure, such as a teddy bear or a person
- Paper cut-outs of clothing that will fit the cardboard doll
- Clear contact paper
- Pieces of adhesive Velcro

SUGGESTIONS
- Enclose the doll and clothing pieces in clear contact paper in order to prolong their life. Attach pieces of Velcro to the front of the doll and back of the clothes so that the clothes will stay on the doll.
- For a child having difficulty naming the clothing, have the child point to different pieces as you name them.
- After a child places a piece of clothing on the doll, ask her to point to the same piece of clothing on herself.
- Talk about the weather being hot, cold, or rainy as you use the appropriate pieces of clothing (e.g., shorts, jacket, or raincoat).

Activity 50: Clothing Name Game

Present two or three photographs of clothing to a child and direct the child to point to a particular piece of clothing in the photo by asking, "Where is the (clothing name)?" Then ask the child to name the clothing herself. If the child does not say the name, repeat the name and encourage the child to imitate the word. Reinforce any attempt that approximates the desired word, including just the beginning sound or a sign for the clothing. Repeat this process by asking another child to point to a different piece of clothing in one of the other photographs. Another variation of this game is to show the child a doll wearing some clothing, such as a shirt, diaper, socks, or hat. Then, proceed as described above.

OBJECTIVES
- Increase recognition and use of the names for common pieces of clothing; and
- Increase verbalization.

EQUIPMENT/SUPPLIES
- Photographs of clothing such as a shirt, pants, a dress, socks, shoes, pajamas, a hat, gloves, or a jacket
- Doll and doll clothing

SUGGESTIONS
- Make your own picture cards by taking photographs of pieces of clothing.
- After a child identifies a piece of clothing in a photograph or on a doll, ask her to point to the same piece of clothing on herself.
- As you show weather-related or seasonal pieces of clothing, talk about the weather being rainy, cold, or hot when one wears that piece of clothing.

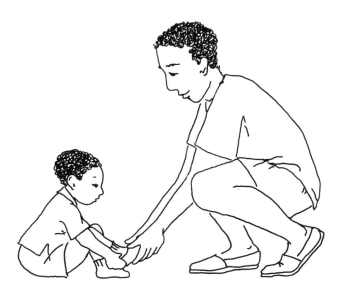

SELF-CARE

Activity 51: Socks and Shoes Practice

In preparation for participating in the program session or a particular activity, direct the child to remove his shoes and socks. Break the activity into steps. Make your verbal directions simple, emphasizing the primary words: "shoes," "socks," "on," "off," "feet," and "toes." With verbal and physical cues/assistance, encourage the child to participate as much as possible in performing the various steps. For example, a child may be able to remove his shoes if they are first untied. Another child may need you to move the shoe past her heel before she can remove the shoe. Similarly, you may need to slide the sock over a child's heel, but then the child can pull the sock off the rest of the way. Later, at an appropriate time, direct the child to put his socks and shoes back on. Follow a similar process as described above to promote the child's maximal participation. For instance, you may pull the sock over the child's toes and next ask the child to pull the sock up the rest of the way. Additionally, you might place the shoe over the child's toes but have him finish putting the shoe on.

OBJECTIVES
- Improve praxis related to self-care skills;
- Increase the ability to participate in putting on and removing shoes and socks;
- Increase the understanding and use of words associated with putting on and taking off socks and shoes;
- Enhance body percept; and
- Improve fine motor coordination.

EQUIPMENT/SUPPLIES
- The child's shoes and socks

SUGGESTIONS
- Talk with the child's family about how to reinforce development of this self-care skill at home.
- Help the child learn to recognize his own shoes by talking about the color and size of his shoes compared with another pair of shoes.

Activity 52: Dress-Up

Dress-up play can be presented in a variety of ways, ranging from structured to free-form, depending upon the goal of the day's activity. The most structured way is to have a child put on a few pieces of clothing (e.g., shirt, hat, and gloves) in front of a full-length mirror. Ask the child questions such as "What is this?" and "Where does this go?" Encourage the child to respond with words and/or gestures. Assist the child as needed with orienting the clothing correctly and doing the fasteners. To promote creativity and socialization, display a variety of clothing and accessories in an area with a full-length mirror and play furniture, such as a table and chairs. Encourage the children to engage in a play scenario, such as getting dressed to go to a party, or getting dressed for a cold day. Facilitate conversation about the clothing, body parts, and the children's play actions. Encourage the children to interact with each other as they pretend to be eating at a restaurant or celebrating a birthday.

OBJECTIVES

- Develop motor planning, sequencing, and coordination related to dressing;
- Enhance body percept;
- Improve independence in dressing;
- Increase awareness and the use of clothing names;
- Increase sharing and turn-taking; and
- Enhance creativity and pretend play.

EQUIPMENT/SUPPLIES

- Assortment of clothes including ones of various textures and with different fasteners (e.g., zippers, snaps, laces, Velcro, and buttons of various sizes)
- Weather-dependent clothing and accessories, such as jackets, hats, gloves, scarves, purses, and jewelry
- Full-length mirror
- Play furniture and dishes

SUGGESTIONS

- For a child having difficulty putting clothes on the correct body parts, touch the body part as you say, "Put it here."
- Grade verbal and physical cues/assistance according to the child's skill with fasteners.
- For a child with sequencing problems, show her photographs of clothes in the correct order for putting on and taking off the clothes.
- Encourage the understanding and use of descriptors ("blue," "soft" or "big"), action words ("zip" or "button"), prepositions ("on" or "off"), and directional adverbs ("up" or "down").
- Have the child choose the appropriate clothes to wear for a particular type of weather, such as a cold day.
- Increase tactile and proprioceptive awareness by encouraging the child to put on or take off clothes without using a mirror.

Activity 53: Hand Washing

Before eating a snack or after participating in hand-dirtying play, have the child wash her hands in the following way. Instruct the child to wet her hands thoroughly with warm water. Use enough soap to work up a lather. Be sure the child washes the palms, backs of the hands, wrists, and between the fingers. Have the child rinse her hands thoroughly. Finally, direct the child to dry her hands completely with a clean paper towel.

OBJECTIVES

- Increase awareness of the steps to hand washing;
- Improve the ability to wash the hands independently;
- Increase sensory awareness of the hands and fingers; and
- Develop the habit of washing the hands at appropriate times.

EQUIPMENT/SUPPLIES

- Soap and dispenser
- Basins or sink
- Paper towels

SUGGESTIONS

- Use basins on a table to introduce this activity.
- Talk about the names of the body parts and actions.
- Have the child use a soft scrub brush to wash her hands.

SELF-CARE
Activity 54: Baby Doll Bath

Place the wash basins filled with a small amount of water (1½ inches deep) on top of towels or inside a plastic wading pool. Place dolls and washing supplies nearby. Demonstrate actions, such as putting foam soap on the doll, brushing or rubbing the "skin," and washing and combing the doll's hair. Talk about your actions and name the doll's body parts. Encourage the children to wash the dolls themselves, talk about the activity, take turns, and share the dolls and supplies.

OBJECTIVES
- Increase awareness of the sequence for taking a bath;
- Increase understanding and the use of names for body parts and action words for washing and grooming;
- Improve body percept;
- Improve fine motor skills;
- Improve interaction, sharing, and turn-taking; and
- Increase tolerance of various tactile experiences.

EQUIPMENT/SUPPLIES
- Waterproof dolls
- Plastic basins
- Shaving cream or foam soap
- Surgical scrub brushes, wash cloths, and sponges
- Small hair brushes or combs
- Water
- Towels
- Plastic wading pool

SUGGESTIONS
- To reduce the cleanup, you might do this outside, weather permitting. Also, you could have the children wear paint smocks or waterproof aprons.
- Sing a song to describe the child's actions, such as "This is the way we wash our hands, wash our hands, wash our hands," to the tune of "Here We Go 'Round The Mulberry Bush."
- Encourage the child to put foam soap on her own arm or leg, scrub the area, and then wipe it off.

Activity 55: Teeth Brushing

Pour about ½-inch of flavored water into a small cup. Dip the end of the toothbrush into the cup. Encourage the child to hold the toothbrush and brush the tongue, teeth, inside of the cheeks, and roof of the mouth. Afterwards, rinse the brush with clean water and let it dry.

OBJECTIVES

- Decrease tactile sensitivity;
- Increase awareness of the mouth structures and their names;
- Improve tongue movement; and
- Increase the ability and willingness to brush the teeth.

EQUIPMENT/SUPPLIES

- Small toothbrushes
- Flavored water (one part juice or non-sugar drink to three parts water)
- Small cups
- Paper towels

SUGGESTIONS

- Give a toothbrush to each child and place the child's name on it.
- Have paper towels ready to wipe up spills.
- Sing, "This is the way we brush our teeth, brush our teeth, brush our teeth, This is the way we brush our teeth early in the morning," to the tune of "Here We Go 'Round The Mulberry Bush."
- For a child who refuses to use a toothbrush, encourage him to use a cotton swab or toothbrush training implement (such as those made by NUK).
- For a reluctant child, playfully try to introduce the toothbrush, swab, or training implement by touching it to her lips. Gradually place it inside her mouth.

CHAPTER 4

Program Management: How to Make it Work

Katherine Newton Inamura, M.A., OTR
Patricia S. Webster, M.A., O
Zoe Mailloux, M.A., OTR, FAOTA
Terri Chew Nishimura, M.A., OTR
Victoria McGuire, B.S. Ed.

For the Milestones program, as with any group therapy program, the staff has had to consider how to facilitate the flow and dynamics of the program; in other words, "how to make it work." Dealing with a number of children, parents, and other staff members simultaneously can be a challenge for therapists and other specialists experienced in working with children on an individual basis. Obviously, the staff must function as a team, and the team should draw on the particular strengths of each member. The staff joins with the families to meet the needs of the individual children and the group as a whole.

Alertness, responsiveness, and consistency tempered with flexibility are important attributes of staff members working in this kind of program. The staff needs these characteristics to anticipate or at least recognize problems and concerns as they arise, relative to management of the group program. The staff must address important management issues including session flow, the individual needs of child and parent, health and safety, socialization and independence, documentation, and interaction with other professionals and the community.

Session Flow

Numerous aspects of the program organization contribute to the flow or progression of each session, including staff preparation, program routine, repetition, transition signals, limited waiting periods, group size, and centers. These program characteristics assist the children in developing greater organization of their behavior. Over time, the children typically increase their attention span, ability to complete activities, and adaptability to transitions and other changes. As a result, the desired, comfortable but lively rhythm of a session is more frequently achieved and maintained, and the session flows smoothly.

Staff Preparation

An important part of adequate staff preparation is the establishment of a team approach. Open communication between staff members is particularly important. Prior to beginning the program and as different situations arise, staff members should discuss and reach an understanding about what their roles will be. Regular or periodic staff meetings allow opportunities for the staff to agree on solutions to problems related to a certain child or the daily routine. The staff must be flexible and recognize that as the children, parents, and staff members participating in the group change, the dynamics of the group change. What worked in the past may not work for the current group. Some change in the routine, approach, or role delineation may be necessary to improve the functioning of the group. In addition to the routine staff meetings, an annual program review by the staff can be a useful forum for considering the staff's observations, the families' feedback, and interactions with the community resources. Such a review can generate additional ideas for strengthening various aspects of the program.

Planning the activities, equipment, and materials to be used during a program session helps increase the effectiveness and efficiency of the staff. However, this planning provides just a general framework for interactions with the children and their families. For each child, the exact course of the interaction and manner in which the equipment and materials are used is guided by the needs of that child and family.

The use of the monthly concepts provides a focus for the selection of activities, equipment, and snack foods and beverages. It also is helpful in creating suggestions for those parents who would like to learn which activities they can carry out at home to foster a particular aspect of their child's development. For example, the staff might suggest having the child find red fruit at the grocery store and play with red play dough at home, during the month when *red* is emphasized in the program.

In the Milestones program, the monthly concepts are selected at least one month in advance. When determining the monthly concepts, the time of year and occurrence of holidays are considered. A record of the previous year's monthly concepts and activities is kept for reference.

During a monthly planning meeting, the staff decides upon the concepts for the upcoming month and chooses the particular activities to enhance the learning of the concepts and achievement of other developmental goals. For each week the staff selects simple craft activities, tabletop activities (e.g., specific toys such as plastic interlocking blocks), tactile medium for a pool, equipment for the Sensory Motor Integration and Gross Motor/Language Centers, songs, and Movement to Music activities.

The Milestones staff also has found it helpful to spend thirty minutes in preparation before each program session. By setting out the materials and equipment before beginning a particular day's session, the staff is able to make smoother and quicker transitions between the different activity periods. The staff also may use this time to coordinate the team's actions in regard to special events (e.g., holiday celebrations) or a problem that has arisen. After the session, the team has another thirty minutes in which to clean up and put away the equipment and materials. Also, the staff discusses the children's responses to that session in particular and to the program over time.

Program Routine

To promote the children's abilities to interact in the most organized and productive way with the objects and people in the program's environment, a daily schedule is followed faithfully but not rigidly to the minute. The use of a schedule creates a routine that enables the children to learn the type of activities that will come next and the associated, expected behavior. Exceptions to this routine are made occasionally to allow for special events.

Each Milestones session begins with an Exploratory Play period, which is the least-structured time period. This allows the children time to adjust to separation from the parent (if that occurs) and to being in the group setting before being required to sit and pay attention for an extended period. During the time spent at the centers, the small groups of children alternate when possible between centers that usually require them to sit and perform a directed activity and those that allow more freedom of movement and choice of activity.

Repetition, Transition Signals, and Limited Waiting Periods

Other features that foster the children's organization of behavior and learning include repetition, transition signals, and short waiting periods. Repetition of some of the activities, toys, and equipment over a week provides the children with some familiarity with the stimulation and more than one opportunity to integrate that stimulation and produce appropriate responses. Additional opportunities give the children a chance to overcome reluctance or apprehension, to take part in the sensory experiences more extensively, and to try out different ways of playing with the materials and objects.

In the Milestones program, most of the transitions are accompanied by definite signals of the impending change. Songs are sung to mark the transition from Exploratory Play to the centers, from Snack Time to Circle Time, and from the program to home. The leaders of the Cognitive/ Language and Pre-speech/Pre-feeding Centers end each group's time at their center by having each child say and/or wave "bye-bye." The children at the other centers know that it is time to move on when the children from another center approach their center. The instruction to wash their hands signals to the children that Snack Time will follow. At Snack Time, the children are taught to show that they are ready to leave the table by finishing their snack and placing their napkin, plate, and cup in the basin. When a child is assisted in putting socks and shoes back on, she knows the day's session will soon be over. The session's end is indicated by the singing of the "Good-bye Song."

Because most children of this age group have difficulty waiting, prolonged periods of inactivity are avoided. For this reason, materials and equipment are set up before the program session begins. The amount of materials, toys, and equipment set out is calculated to encourage the children to learn to wait brief periods, but not to frustrate them excessively by requiring extended waiting periods. The time that the children spend waiting in line to wash their hands is reduced by dividing the large group into two smaller ones that use different restrooms. Additionally, a child is permitted to get up from the snack table when he has finished his snack and put away his dishes and trash.

Group Size

It is important for the staff of any group program to consider optimal and maximal numbers of participants. The Milestones staff has determined twelve to sixteen children to be the maximum for the current physical setting. Frequently, the number of children in attendance on a particular day may be less because of illness or other appointments. Even with fewer children present, the level of activity may become intense at times because of the age and functional level of the children and the total number of people in the room.

The Exploratory Play period is a time in which a multitude of activities may be occurring simultaneously. Therefore, a book area is available for those children wanting a quieter and less busy area. In addition, during the Exploratory Play period some children may choose to go into the Sensory Motor Integration Center. There they engage in activities providing tactile, proprioceptive, and vestibular sensory input that, in turn, may help them organize their behavior. Another means of preventing the program session from becoming too chaotic is the division of the large group into smaller groups for the centers.

Centers

Many group programs use "centers" or small-group activities to address specific developmental areas or tasks. A smaller group size permits the center leader to give more focused attention to each child relative to the therapeutic activities and reduces the competing stimuli.

At the centers of the Milestones program, the assistance of a second person (volunteer, parent, occupational or physical therapy student, or another staff member) often is helpful or even required. Because of the safety issues, two staff members direct the activities at the Sensory Motor Integration and Gross Motor/Language centers. Assistance for other centers depends on the availability of a helper and the behaviors of the children within the small group. The leaders of the Cognitive/Language and Pre-speech/Pre-feeding centers may choose activities that some group members can perform independently while the leader and the helper work with other children individually. Children spend ten minutes at one center in Milestones. This has been found to be the maximum amount of time that many children want and are able to attend to activities at one center.

Individual Needs of Child and Family

The unique needs and values of each child and family should always be addressed as much as possible within the therapeutic group environment. The Milestones staff discovers the needs and values of each child and family through discussions, reports, and observation. The staff and parents work together to aid a child's adjustment to the group setting/routine and maximize the benefits the child and family gain from program participation. There may be modification in the stimulation, addition of other intervention services, and/or adaptations to meet the family's needs and values.

Adjustment to Group Setting and Routine

One of the first ways a child demonstrates individuality is her reaction to being in a group setting and to separating from her parent (if that occurs). Therefore, the staff of a group program needs to determine how it will handle separation difficulties as well as what options will be available for family involvement. In the Milestones program, the staff attempts to discover what approach will help each child adjust to the group. Some children have a very strong need for a parent to be present to provide a base of security and act as an intermediary for interactions with the staff and other children. They require physical contact or close proximity to the parent. Such children may require several months of acclimation before they can accept direction from the staff, with or without the parent present. Therefore, the parent has to assume the roles of teacher and therapist. The Milestones staff assists the parents by modeling interactions with other children and providing verbal instructions and suggestions.

A number of children will observe at first before gradually being drawn into direct interaction with the toys, equipment, staff, and peers. For a child who is very upset and whose parent is unable to attend with him, one staff member may take responsibility for comforting the child by holding him and possibly taking the child from the group setting into another room to calm him by rocking or swinging.

In some cases, a child is resistant to trying new, independent behaviors when the parent is present. Discussing such a situation with the parent and mutually deciding on a plan of action usually provides the best solution. It might include having the staff model interactions that encourage the child to try new experiences, and the parent attempting to adjust his interactions with his child. Another option might be that the parent would leave the setting at least for part of each program session.

On rare occasions, a child may be unable to adjust to the group setting even after a few weeks of attendance. The staff, the child's case manager, and the parents may jointly conclude that the child is not ready for the group setting. In that case, the child is withdrawn from the program. If the child's adjustment difficulties appear related to poor sensory integration, the staff may suggest that the child receive individual physical or occupational therapy using a sensory integration treatment approach to improve the child's tolerance of a multisensory setting. In other settings, other forms of therapeutic intervention might be available. It may be appropriate for the child to try participation in the group program at a later date.

Modifications in the Stimulation

The monitoring and adjustment of the types and amounts of sensory stimuli that children receive during a group program can have an impact on how well they function in the setting. Some children benefit from the addition, reduction, or alteration of sensory stimulation. In Milestones, the staff often provides extra touch pressure and motion stimulation to disorganized, distractible, and/or hyperactive children. Such children might be encouraged to spend time in the Sensory Motor Integration Center during the Exploratory Play time period or allowed to spend an extra period in this center rather than going to the Cognitive/Language Center.

Occasionally, a child will wear a weighted vest, as this type of proprioceptive sensory input may help a child better organize his behavior. The staff may use tactile-proprioceptive cues (e.g., pressure down through the shoulders or head) and/or verbal reminders for children having difficulty remaining seated and attentive during Circle Time. For some children, these cues and the visual/tactile cues of the carpet pieces are not enough. They are better able to focus their attention and remain seated for a longer period of time if they sit in a chair with an attached tray (see Figure 2-12). Typically, these same children also sit in these chairs for the Cognitive/Language and Pre-speech/Pre-feeding Centers.

Another example of modifying the stimulation or activity would be guiding a child through the motions to activate a toy or perform actions to a song. In another instance, a staff member may position a distractible child so that there are no children or toys in front of her except for the toy being presented. For a child with limited hearing or very delayed expressive language, the staff may use sign language or a communication book. Similarly, the staff may add auditory and tactile cues and materials for a child with limited vision. Likewise, the staff may simplify a gross motor activity for a child with limited mobility.

Occasionally, the Milestone staff realizes that a quiet, passive child may not be getting sufficient individual attention, particularly during the Exploratory Play periods, because of the demands of active and/or aggressive children. In such a case, the staff will make a concentrated effort to focus on the quiet child's performance and facilitate it as needed.

Need for Individual Therapy or Other Services

Consideration of the need for other specialized or individualized help often may be appropriate for children attending a therapeutic early intervention program. The children who are referred to Milestones

Reporter
Consumer of Information
Decision Maker
Development Facilitator in the Home and Community
Participant in Parent Meetings
Participant in Program Sessions
  Observer
  Development Facilitator
  Program/Clinic Helper

Figure 4-1   The Roles of Family Members

have received varying amounts of professional intervention. Some are receiving individual occupational or physical therapy at the time of the referral. Depending on need, the child may either continue receiving individual therapy at the same or reduced frequency, or discontinue the individual therapy.

Other referred children have been monitored only by periodic developmental assessments or they are new clients to the referring agency. In some cases, after a child begins participation in Milestones, the staff or the child's family concludes that a child would benefit from individual occupational, physical, or speech therapy. The staff and parents discuss that possibility and then may make that recommendation to the referring agency. This agency may concur with the recommendation and fund the additional service. Occasionally, there are children who are receiving other services (such as behavioral management or vision therapy) from outside agencies. The Milestones staff attempts to coordinate its efforts with these other professionals.

Family Needs

Family members, particularly parents, usually assume a variety of roles relative to their young children's participation in any group program (see Figure 4-1). These roles in relation to the Milestones program were introduced in Chapter 2. As stated there, the families decide what level of direct participation in the group sessions best meets their needs as well as those of their child.

In addition to those parents unable to attend regularly due to work outside the home or other commitments, a parent may choose to attend infrequently because he needs some time away from the child. Also, a parent may believe that the child needs to learn to feel comfortable without the parent present. A parent may make this decision when first placing the child in the program or decide this after the child has been in the program for a while. The Milestones staff recognizes that these needs are valid and provides support to make the separation possible.

A number of parents may desire to take on the roles of teacher and therapist at least part of the time during the group sessions, even if their children respond well to interactions with staff members. The staff encourages this because parents who take on these roles in the group program may be better able to incorporate these roles into the home setting.

In some cases, a parent wishes to participate actively in the group session but has no one to care for a sibling during the program time. In that circumstance, the sibling might be allowed to participate with the parent for parts of the program session, as long as he is not disruptive to the group. The most feasible time periods for this to occur are the Exploratory Play period and Circle Time. The sibling and parent might wait in the waiting room for the rest of the session.

A parent also might choose to be an observer. The reasons for this might include a desire to have a respite from direct interaction, to watch how her child interacts with others, or to observe how others guide her child's play.

Multicultural Diversity

As will be the case for many early intervention programs, the children attending Milestones come from varying ethnic backgrounds. Some belong to families that have recently immigrated to the United States. Others belong to families that have been long-time residents but have maintained strong ties to their ethnic culture. Numerous other children have less defined ethnic backgrounds.

A family's ethnic background, whether well identified or more ambiguous, influences its values and attitudes. In every case, a family's attitudes and values about medicine, intervention, health, disability, play, independence, and family participation affect the family's goals for a child and acceptance of particular interventions. Knowledge of values and beliefs held by various cultures can help staff understand the decisions and responses of family members. For example, the staff noticed that some Hispanic parents seemed reluctant to have their children remove their shoes during the program. A staff member familiar with Hispanic culture suggested that the parents might be fearful that by being barefoot, their children might more easily catch a cold. With this understanding, the staff discussed with the parents the reasons for removing the shoes (i.e., to increase the child's tactile perception with her feet and to prevent slipping when climbing on equipment). The staff and parents reached an agreement to leave the children's socks on when the weather was cool. In another instance, an Asian parent commented that it was unusual that the children were encouraged to play in uncooked rice. Another staff member, knowing the importance of rice as food in the Asian culture, understood what led to her statement. In this case, the parent did not appear to desire a change in the intervention method, but would not have wanted to carry out this activity in the family's home.

Thus, even when goals and objectives have been set collaboratively by family and staff, the families may demonstrate some discomfort with or ask questions about particular aspects of the program. The staff needs to be alert to signs of unease and sensitive to what concerns may be behind the parent's distress and questions. Discussion by staff and parents can help resolve the matter by increasing mutual understanding and by leading to program adaptations appropriate to the child and family.

When a parent and child are not proficient in English, it is optimal to have a bilingual speaker to facilitate clear and meaningful communication.

This person could be another family member, family friend, or staff member. The assistance of an interpreter is especially helpful at critical times, such as entry to the program, developmental assessments, progress reviews, and discharge.

One member of the Milestones staff speaks Spanish, which is the primary language of most of the referred families who have limited English proficiency. In these cases, she is the main verbal communicator with the families. She also will speak Spanish to these children to assist their development of cognitive and language skills. The other staff members may learn a few words of Spanish or other languages to motivate the children and exchange social pleasantries with the parents; otherwise, they will use one- or two-word phrases in English as well as nonverbal communication in their interactions.

Socialization and Independence

Two issues with which all toddlers struggle are socialization and independence. The children have to learn how to act independently in exploring the world and yet behave appropriately in social interactions. For many children in Milestones, participation in this group setting is their first regular contact with other people in a structured situation outside of their home. As discussed earlier, the staff assists the children in becoming comfortable in the group setting and being comfortable in the absence of the parent, if that occurs. Even if a parent wants to participate regularly in the group program, often it is an appropriate goal for both child and parent to be able to tolerate occasional separation for at least a thirty- to sixty-minute period.

Self-Awareness and Self-Help

The staff encourages a child to learn that he is a separate being from others, has freedom to act independently at times, and is responsible for his actions. These goals can be fostered by various means. One simple way of encouraging independence is to have an individual basket or box in which each child can place her belongings. The basket or box displays the child's name and photograph for easy recognition. During a Milestones session, the opening song for Circle Time is "Here We are Together," which identifies each child by name. Other songs that recognize the children individually may also be sung periodically.

During Exploratory Play, the children are encouraged to choose their own toys and activities. A staff member will provide verbal and physical prompting if a child has difficulty choosing and engaging in appropriate play with toys and activities. After playing with a toy, the child is encouraged to put it back on the shelf. At the transition to Circle Time, the children are directed to pick up a carpet piece from a pile and carry it (with assistance if needed) to the circle area. At the completion of Circle Time, the children carry their mats back to the pile.

When a child enters the program setting, she is assisted in removing her shoes and socks. While removing them and putting them back on, she is taught the steps so that she can become as independent as possible in this task. Later in the session, each child is taught the necessary steps of hand washing. Independence also is encouraged at Snack Time. Each child is aided only to the degree necessary, when drinking from a cup, eating with fingers, and feeding himself with a spoon. After a child has finished his snack, he places the trash and dirty dishes into a basin. At the end of the session, each child is directed to find his own basket and retrieve his belongings.

Communication and Cooperation

In addition to learning to tolerate separation from their parents, young children are learning to communicate their needs and desires to others and to cooperate with others during activities. To facilitate this form of independence, staff members of early intervention programs should encourage the children to communicate with them nonverbally (e.g., gestures or sign language) and/or verbally (e.g., words or word approximations) rather than anticipate all of the children's wants and needs. A child with very limited expressive communication might be taught to use a simple communication board or book of photographs to indicate his desires. Children also should be encouraged to ventilate frustrations verbally, not physically.

During the sessions, the children are helped over time to progress from parallel play to more interactive play. The program activities are designed to encourage interactions between children, turn-taking, and the sharing of toys and equipment. For example, more than one bucket and shovel or other toy will be placed in a pool of rice to encourage two or three children to play simultaneously. A staff member may further promote interaction by suggesting that the children take turns hiding a toy for the others to find.

Self-Discipline

To facilitate the children's learning to monitor their own behavior (i.e., self-discipline), the staff and parents can model appropriate behavior, state clearly and simply what behavior is desired, praise "good" behavior, and be consistent about what behavior is expected. In Milestones, the children are not allowed to hurt themselves, others, or property. If a child is behaving in an undesired or unsafe manner, the inappropriate behavior is identified (e.g., "No throwing."). An alternate activity may be suggested and demonstrated (e.g., "Put the blocks in."). If the frequency or intensity of a child's misbehavior is causing significant disruption to the group, the situation is discussed with the family members and an approach to the problem agreed upon. One option would be to provide the child with additional sensory experiences (such as firm-touch pressure or slow, rhythmic movement) to enable him to respond more appropriately to the group environment. Another possibility would be the use of time-outs as a consequence of the undesired behavior.

A time-out involves isolating the child for a specific time to give her a chance to calm down and regain control of her behavior. When the child misbehaves, a staff member or parent identifies the misbehavior (e.g., "No pushing.") and indicates to the child that she will have some time alone "to think about how to play nicely" or to "calm down." The child will then stay in a certain spot, such as a chair turned away from the other children, for a specific time. The period might last only thirty to sixty seconds. After the time period is over or the child has calmed down sufficiently, she is allowed to rejoin the other children. If the child demonstrates the misbehavior again, the time-out is repeated. The staff and parents always make an effort to notice and praise the child's appropriate behavior.

In some cases, the children who are very physically aggressive toward others also may be receiving behavioral therapy. Often it is helpful to have the behavioral therapist observe the child in the group setting. At the very least, the Milestones staff exchanges information with the behavioral therapist and coordinates efforts to reduce inappropriate behavior.

Health and Safety

Health and safety are significant issues for any group program for children. Appropriate policies and procedures have to be established and followed concerning the occurrence of illness, the presence of medical conditions, and safety precautions.

Illness

When a child begins the program, the parent receives a copy of the Program Parent Handbook (see Appendix A), which contains the program policies and procedures. Within the policies and procedures are a request that the child's immunizations be up to date and a list of health-related conditions for which a child should be kept home from the program (e.g., known contagious diseases or open wounds). When a child becomes ill (e.g., develops a fever or diarrhea) during a session, the child is sent home if possible. If no one is available to take the child home early, a staff member stays with the child in isolation until the end of the program session. The parent is notified by telephone, in person, or in writing, of the observed symptoms of illness.

If a child exhibits a skin rash, marked loss of hair in one area, unusual bruising, or other possible signs of a medical condition, abuse, or neglect, the program director will discuss the staff's observations with the parent. The director will try to determine whether the parent is displaying appropriate concern and actions, such as taking the child to see a physician. Additionally, the staff may contact the child's case manager from the referring agency about any concerns.

In cases of potentially reportable contagious diseases not being treated, the staff will report the situation to the local department of health and the child will be excluded from the program until the condition has been diagnosed and treated appropriately. If the staff has reason to suspect abuse or neglect, the program director will report the suspicion to the appropriate local authorities as required by law.

Medical Conditions

The staffs of most early intervention group programs will want to develop or use a procedure to identify medical background information about the children before they enter the program. Typically, the Milestones staff receives some medical history of the child from the referring agency. Additional medical information is obtained by having the family complete the Child and Family Information Questionnaire (see Appendix B). On this sheet the parent is asked to provide information about the child's medical status (i.e., medical diagnosis, occurrence of seizures, medications, allergies, and conditions affecting activity). If the parent reports that the child experiences seizures, the parent also must complete a Seizure Information Sheet (see Appendix F). Because it is the program's policy for the children to have up-to-date immunizations, the staff requests verification of immunizations. Also, the staff asks whether the child has any difficulty eating certain foods or drinking liquids. From the Child and Family Information Questionnaire, medical records, and other information the parent supplies, the staff can determine whether any particular precautions or modifications in activities are necessary.

Control of Contagious Diseases and Infection

All early intervention program staff will want to use standard precautions to control disease and infection. To reduce the spread of contagious diseases, the Milestones staff follows certain procedures. If a child mouths a toy, the toy is placed aside for later disinfection. Each child is given his own toothbrush to use during oral motor activities for the length of his participation in Milestones. Other equipment that is used in or around one child's mouth is not used by another child until it has been cleaned and dried. For example, each child would have his own blowpipe for use during that session. The blowpipes would be cleaned before reuse. A staff member uses gloves if she will be placing her fingers inside a child's mouth for oral stimulation. Both staff and children wash their hands before Snack Time.

If a diaper needs to be changed, a staff member wears gloves and changes the child's diaper on a mat that is disinfected afterward. Occasionally a child is being toilet trained at home and the staff will reinforce the toilet training during the program. An adapter seat is placed on an adult-size toilet for the child to use. Only the adapter seat has to be disinfected immediately, eliminating the need to clean a waste receptacle. For any incident involving blood, vomit, or other body fluid of a significant amount, staff members use gloves and masks as a precautionary measure.

Safety

When a child begins the program, the program director informs the family in more detail about the nature of the program activities and type of therapy equipment and materials, and possible risks and benefits of participation. A parent should sign a form indicating an understanding of the risks and consent for the child's participation in the program activities.

While the children are interacting with the toys and equipment, the staff monitors the children for their response to the stimulation and the safety of their actions. As needed, the staff will alter an activity to optimize the amount of stimulation or to avert injury.

The staff teaches safety precautions. For example, the children are instructed not to throw toys, except for balls and bean bags in certain areas. The staff members verbally and physically guide the children in mounting and dismounting equipment safely. The children are cautioned to watch out for other children and equipment as they are playing on and around the equipment.

Documentation

Documentation is a means for tracking a child's responses to the intervention services and reporting on the child's progress to the family, referral source, and other professionals. Documentation can alert the staff to how well the services fit the needs of the child and family.

Weekly Notes

Once a child begins the Milestones program, a note is written weekly about the child's responses to the group setting and progress relative to sensory integration and other developmental abilities. From week to week, different staff members write about the child so that they can share their varied perspectives on the child's behaviors. However, the staff member writing the note on a particular day consults other staff members about current observations of the child.

Goals and Objectives

The Milestones staff and parents jointly decide on goals and objectives for the child to achieve during program participation. They establish the goals and objectives for the first six months by the thirtieth day of the child's participation or the sixth program session attended by the child. The goals and objectives are based on observations of the child, previously identified strengths and weaknesses of the child (some of these would have been established by the referring agency's developmental assessment of the child), and parental concerns. Typically, four to five developmental domains are addressed. The goals may be directed toward improvement in the following domains: organization of behavior, sensory processing, gross motor, fine motor, cognition, socialization, language or communication, and self-care. Some of the objectives may be based on items from the

Early Intervention Developmental Profile (EIDP) (Rogers and D'Eugenio 1981; Rogers et al. 1981) (see Appendix G for a sample page). A staff member records the goals and objectives (see the case examples in Chapter 5), and the parents and referral source are provided with copies. At the parent's request, copies are sent to other professionals.

Developmental Assessment

Many developmental assessments are available to early intervention programs. Case-Smith (1997) indicates that it is important to consider the nature of the children being served and the planned use of the evaluation results when selecting an evaluation instrument. Additional factors that may affect the choice are the background of the staff and requirements of the funding agency.

When appropriate, the Milestones staff administers the EIDP every five to six months of program attendance or at other selected intervals. This evaluation tool was selected because it assesses abilities up to thirty-six months of age and provides a hierarchy of skills in commonly considered developmental domains. Although a staff member can mark some test items on the basis of the child's performance within the group, he administers most of the test items with the child in isolation, in order to obtain the child's best performance. The parents often are consulted about their child's skills, particularly in reference to the Social/Emotional and Self-care sections.

The EIDP manual states that the highest-ranking items passed in each developmental domain should be the ones reported to indicate a child's potential. However, because many of the Milestones children demonstrate a wide range of scores in the passed items, the staff reports the developmental level at which the child is passing the majority of items, as well as the developmental level at which the child is demonstrating established and emerging skills.

In addition to the fact that the scatter of scores sometimes misrepresents a child's true functional level, other weaknesses of this assessment are that it is not standardized and it may not be familiar to personnel from schools and other service agencies. As with other developmental evaluations, the number of items for receptive and expressive language at certain developmental levels is meager. When a more definitive assessment of language abilities is needed, the speech-language pathologist may administer the *Receptive-Expressive Emergent Language Test* (Bzoch and League 1991).

Progress Reports

Progress notes typically are written at about six-month intervals. Before writing the report, the staff pools information about the child's responses to the program, developmental gains, areas of continued concern, and the possible need for other intervention services. Additionally, a staff member meets with the parent(s) to exchange observations about the child's progress in the program, changes in the child's behavior at home or in the community, and developmental abilities requiring facilitation within the program or, potentially, from other types of intervention. If the staff has performed a developmental evaluation, the staff representative reports those results to the parent(s). If the child will be continuing in the program, the parent(s) and staff member establish another set of goals and objectives for the child's next six months of participation. In the case of a child who will become thirty-six months of age during the upcoming six months, the staff informs the parent(s) about the transition meeting (as described in Chapter 2) that will occur when the child is thirty to thirty-three months old.

After meeting with the parent(s), a staff member writes the progress note. It includes an indication of the child's success in meeting goals and objectives and brief statements about the child's strengths and areas of concern. If developmental testing has been performed, results are reported. At the end of the note, the staff member makes recommendations about continuance in the program, addition of other services (e.g., individual occupational, physical, or speech therapy), or type of school placement. If the child is expected to continue in the program, new goals and objectives are attached to the report. Copies of the progress report are provided to the parents, referral source, and other professionals as indicated by the parents.

Interactions with Other Professionals and the Community

Depending on a variety of factors that include the image and reputation of the facility, the professionals involved in the program, and the funding sources for the clients, interaction with other professionals and agencies in the community can be a critical element in determining the success or failure of an early intervention program. Effective communication and professional interface serve, first and foremost, to ensure that the overall developmental needs of the children are being comprehensively met. In addition, interactions with other professionals can serve to provide support for continuation of a program by promoting ongoing referrals.

Cultivation of Referral Sources

In many cases, it is likely that children will be referred to a program by other professionals. When there is a source of potential clients such as a government agency, local pediatric hospital, community children's health center, or individuals who come in contact with potential group participants (e.g., pediatricians, speech therapists, and early childhood educators), it is helpful for the early intervention program to provide guidelines to facilitate appropriate referrals. Information about appropriate age groups, disabilities, and functional levels, plus specifications such as requirements that the child be toilet trained or ambulatory, can be made available along with information about the program to assist in the pre-selection of admissible participants. Such guidelines also will be helpful to the referring professional because they allow for more appropriate distribution of information to families.

The Milestones staff has created a handout, parent handbook, and other printed materials describing the program. These are disseminated to agencies, hospitals, schools, private practitioners, and parents. Additionally, the staff has made presentations detailing the Milestones program to the referring agencies as well as representatives of agencies, schools, hospitals, and other programs providing early intervention services.

The development of a form or questionnaire also can be useful for ensuring that relevant questions consistently are asked when contact about a potential referral is made. The form may be especially important if the program is likely to have families who contact it directly (e.g., a church-based program) or when it is common for someone other than a program director to record initial information about the child. The Milestones program has a simple form for recording preliminary information (including presenting problems of the child and significant events in the child's medical and developmental history).

Whether or not there are funding ties with the referral source, it is extremely important that the early intervention program be aware of and fulfill the expectations of the referring agency or individual. A referral by a professional is, in many ways, a reflection of that professional. She has expressed a degree of confidence in the program by recommending it. Therefore, it is critical that the needs of the referral source be met if continued referrals are desired. The intervention program needs to be cognizant of the referral source's own goals for the child, the specific service requested or expected, and the feedback or consultation necessary to enhance other types of intervention. If a referring agency also is providing funding for a child, there are likely to be specific expectations concerning the program design, reporting, accounting, and discharge criteria. Agreeing to meet specific requirements tied to funding brings with it the added responsibility of making sure that the child is able to continue to receive the service as needed. In this situation, the program should be prepared to continue services for a child if discontinuation of funding is the result of failure to meet agreed-upon requirements of the referring agency. Ongoing and effective communication is one way to ensure that the overall needs and expectations of the referral source are being consistently met.

Importance of Verbal and Written Reports

In addition to addressing the expectations of a referral source, professional communications serve to coordinate the various services that the children in the group may be receiving. Because other professionals who have an interest in the children of the group may not be able to observe a child on a routine basis, communication becomes especially important. Verbal and written reports often are the main representation of a group program to outside professionals and agencies. As such, special care should be taken to ensure that such reports reflect professional standards. Abbreviated words, phrases, and technical jargon that often are used intraprofessionally should be avoided for interdisciplinary communication.

While a child is attending the program, professional communication plays a role in coordinating services by creating an awareness of current levels of functioning, synchronizing intervention techniques, and offering suggestions for interactions with the child outside of the group. Professional communications also serve to prepare the children and their families for transition out of the group into other programs or school. Transitional and discharge reports also may include home programs, follow-up recommendations, and additional referrals.

The Milestones written reports, as described in the previous section, have evolved over time to reflect the type and amount of information desired by the families, referral sources, and school personnel. Telephone conversations between the Milestones staff and the referring case manager or other professionals continue to be important in relaying and discussing concerns and issues related to a family's program participation. Visits by the case manager or another professional to observe a child in the program also are encouraged to promote a clearer understanding of the child's ability to function in a structured, group setting.

Public Relations and Marketing

Although public relations and marketing are thought of as relevant only for the business world, they also are important in the provision of health-care services. Good public relations, including the image and reputation of an intervention program, help to ensure that children will have access to the appropriate services.

The way in which a community becomes aware of an early intervention program will be determined to a large extent by the type of program and its base of support. Programs that exist within large private hospital settings are likely to have greater access to resources such as graphic design and printing services for brochures and promotional events. Within this type of setting, it is possible to maximize an association with an established community entity. However, smaller, independent programs face a greater challenge in establishing a name, image, and reputation.

Although more and more professional groups are beginning to use advertising, its use is somewhat controversial and uncommon among health-related services for children. As discussed earlier, a brochure or handout can be very helpful in communicating information about a program. For most settings, creating printed material using language that is professional, yet clear and understandable, probably is more important than investing in glossy, elaborate brochures. Although advertisements may be appropriate in certain parent or professional publications, it might be equally or more effective to encourage the writing of articles about the program in these resources. The Ayres Clinic has not found Yellow Page listings to be helpful in generating referrals to its various programs, including Milestones. However, early intervention programs that more appropriately can be listed with preschools may find this medium useful.

As is true with most aspects of public relations, personal contact is an extremely powerful tool. Care should be taken to ensure that initial calls or visits are handled in a friendly, organized, and professional manner. Both verbal and written communications are critical to the impressions that will be formed about the program. Visits to the program also should be planned carefully. The Milestones staff has found it important to limit the number of visitors on any given day, so that the children are not distracted excessively. Some children, at certain stages of their program participation, may not be able to tolerate visitors. Although visitors should not be subjected to an artificial representation of the group program, care should be taken so that they will have an opportunity to observe a true representation and not the worst-case scenario. For the Milestones program, a staff member (usually the director) will accompany visitors during their observations to explain the purpose of various activities and aspects of the routine. Also, the staff member is available to answer visitors' questions and reduce misconceptions that could occur if the visitors are left entirely on their own.

Making personal visits to referral sources and presentations to appropriate community groups can prove very effective for disseminating information about a program. In addition to periodic presentations to current and potential referral sources, staff members represent the program at an annual resource fair for parents and various early intervention service representatives. Ensuring satisfaction for the children and their families is a key element of good public relations. Parents often are the best source of information for other parents, and those who are satisfied usually are anxious to assist others in finding beneficial resources.

SUMMARY

The challenge of creating and maintaining a therapeutic environment in a group setting is often even greater than in a one-on-one situation. The flow and dynamics of a group depend upon a unified team, adequate planning and preparation for each program session, and adaptation to the uniqueness of each child and family. Health/safety and socialization/independence issues also have to be appropriately addressed.

Effective documentation aids the staff in monitoring a child's response to the program's services and sharing that information with the child's family and interested professionals. Effective interaction with other professionals and the community promotes continued referrals, funding, and other support for the program. Also, it fosters better collaboration in the provision of early intervention services.

All of these factors influence the effectiveness of a program to meet the needs of a particular child and family. The following chapter presents the cases of three children and their families who participated in the Milestones program. It illustrates how the Milestones staff worked together with the families to provide appropriate intervention services.

CHAPTER 5

Case Examples: How the Program Worked

Patricia S. Webster, M.A., OTR
Katherine Newton Inamura, M.A., OTR
Victoria McGuire, B.S. Ed.

Each child and family have a unique pattern of personality traits, abilities, and needs, and experience a different family environment and interactions. Each family unit brings to the Milestones experience its own distinctive blend of needs, values, beliefs, and history. Case studies are offered here as examples of how the Milestones program met the challenge of providing service to three unique families. The names and other identifying characteristics of the children have been changed to protect their privacy and that of their families.

Melissa

Melissa was a cute, curly haired girl of mixed racial background. She entered the program at age twenty months. Prior to program entry, she had received in-home physical therapy twice a week through a state agency that referred her to Milestones. Melissa had a history of prenatal exposure to illicit drugs and had been placed in a foster family shortly after birth. Because her foster parents rarely came to the program site, the staff communicated with the family through telephone calls, notes, reports, and newsletters. Melissa was transported to the program by a van funded by the referring state agency.

When Melissa began the program, she was very active and walked independently. She would not remain sitting at a center unless held by an adult. Melissa had difficulty adjusting to the group setting. She would cry or cling to a staff member, off and on, during the entire two-hour session. Melissa had very limited verbal language skills. Melissa's fear of movement on any kind of swing appeared to be related to difficulty processing vestibular information. She did like climbing and was calmed by firm touch pressure and/or slow vestibular input when held by a staff member. Melissa also enjoyed self-imposed proprioceptive input such as falling into large pillows. The staff postulated that her inability to sit for fine motor tasks or group stories and songs was associated with deficient integration of vestibular, proprioceptive, tactile, and visual sensory information.

The staff, with input from the family, set the following goals and objectives for Melissa during her first six months of program attendance.

Initial Program Goals/Objectives

1. Improve organization of behavior as demonstrated by:
   Remaining seated during Circle Time for five minutes, needing no more than two verbal prompts during four sessions.
2. Increase language and communication skills as demonstrated by:
   Increasing spontaneous and prompted vocalizations to five times during twenty-five minutes of Exploratory Play.
3. Improve social skills as demonstrated by:
   Taking a toy from another child no more than one time during each session.
4. Improve independence in self-help skills as demonstrated by:
   Holding a small glass, drinking from the glass, and returning the glass to the table without spilling, three out of five times.

During her program sessions, the staff attempted to normalize Melissa's response to vestibular input by first sitting with Melissa on a platform swing as it was moved. Generally, any vestibular activity was followed by one involving deep touch pressure and/or proprioception such as being held, playing in a container of balls, or rolling in a large pillow. The physical therapist suggested techniques to assist Melissa's weight shifts and balance on moving equipment. At the Pre-speech/Pre-feeding Center, Melissa was encouraged to explore oral motor stimulation with a toothbrush, vibrator, or washcloth. She learned to blow bubbles and imitate sounds. Initially she sat on a staff member's lap during the Cognitive/Language Center, but later she was able to remain sitting in a chair with an attached tray. Melissa learned to attend to short stories, match colors, share toys, and take turns. At Snack Time, she first drank from a small cup with a staff member's hand positioned over hers. She progressed to requiring only verbal cues and eventually to needing no assistance for cup drinking.

After four months of program attendance, Melissa had achieved all but one of her goals. She did not meet Goal 1, which was related to improvement in organization of behavior. At twenty-five months of age, she was administered the *EIDP*. According to this evaluation, Melissa performed at the twelve- to fifteen-month level for language and feeding skills; at the sixteen- to nineteen-month level for perceptual/fine motor, cognitive, dressing, and hygiene skills; and at the twenty- to twenty-three-month level for social-emotional and gross motor skills. Thus, Melissa was demonstrating developmental delays ranging from as little as two to five months to as great as ten to thirteen months.

Melissa attended Milestones for another year until she turned three years old. She continued to make significant improvement with the greatest gains in language, fine motor, and self-help skills. The goals and objectives established for Melissa to achieve during her last six months of participation in the Milestones program were as follows.

Final Program Goals/Objectives

1. Improve organization of behavior as demonstrated by:
   Remaining seated during Circle Time for five minutes, needing no more than two verbal prompts.
2. Improve cognitive skills as demonstrated by:
   a. Imitating a model of three to four blocks.
   b. Matching two sets of shapes.
3. Improve language and communication skills as demonstrated by:
   a. Using three-word sentences.
   b. Responding appropriately to two questions regarding prepositions such as "on" and "in."
4. Increase perceptual/fine motor skills as demonstrated by:
   Copying a circle that is already drawn.
5. Improve motor planning and sensory processing during gross motor play as demonstrated by:
   a. Walking up and down stairs with no support.
   b. Not running in front of a moving piece of equipment.

As the time of her program discharge came near, Melissa was able to meet all of these goals and objectives with the following exception and qualifications. She failed to meet Goal 1 because she continued to need physical prompts to remain seated for five minutes. Also, Melissa did not consistently demonstrate the behaviors described under Goal 5. She could walk up stairs with no support, but touched a wall or rail when going down stairs. Occasionally she would walk or run in front of moving equipment. Improvements included her active participation in vestibular play and her choosing to play on a variety of swings, the merry-go-round, and riding toys. Her need for deep pressure input immediately after these activities decreased. She still tended to be very active, enjoying gross motor play more than fine motor activities that required sitting.

She was administered the *EIDP* again at thirty-four months of age. Melissa's developmental skills were at the thirty-two- to thirty-five-month level in most areas, with language and gross motor skills at the twenty-eight- to thirty-one-month level. She had reduced the gap between her chronological age and developmental skills to zero for most areas and six months for problem areas.

Because of her prenatal exposure to drugs and the remaining developmental delays, Melissa qualified for a preschool program offered by the local public school district for children with developmental delays. With the approval of her foster parents, Melissa began attending that program after leaving the Milestones program. It was reported that she adjusted well to the new environment and continued to make good progress.

Carl

Carl began attending the Milestones program twice a week when he was nineteen months old. He was referred by a state agency providing services to developmentally delayed children. He was an active, curly haired boy of mixed racial background. He had a diagnosis of cerebral palsy and had received in-home physical therapy before entering the Milestones program. His orthopedic needs (ankle-foot orthoses) continued to be monitored periodically by a state agency that provided therapy services in the public schools (a different agency from the one referring Carl to Milestones). Carl was an only child and lived with his natural parents. Both parents participated in the program and attended monthly parent meetings. Carl's mother usually accompanied him to the program sessions. She made friends with other mothers of children in the group and organized an informal support group.

When Carl began the program, he played with toys by throwing and banging them. He demonstrated defensive behavior with most tactile media. Carl required help with spoon-feeding. He could not control the flow of liquid from a cup and frequently spilled the liquid. He demonstrated increased muscle tone, toe walking, and an unsteady gait with frequent falls. He had difficulty with visual space perception, awareness of body position in space, and vestibular processing. He was deficient in praxis, particularly in the execution of movements, due to problems with timing and coordination. His practic difficulties appeared to be related both to his cerebral palsy and the sensory integration deficits noted above. Carl did respond well to proprioceptive input, which seemed to help him organize his motor responses.

The staff and parents agreed upon the following goals and objectives for Carl to work towards in the beginning six-month period.

Initial Program Goals/Objectives
1. Improve cognitive and fine motor skills as demonstrated by:
   a. Placing six pegs into six holes within thirty-five seconds.
   b. Imitating vertical and horizontal strokes with a crayon.
2. Improve language and communication skills as demonstrated by:
   a. Using one word consistently during the program session.
   b. Choosing one object upon request from a choice of two objects or pictures of the objects.
3. Improve gross motor skills as demonstrated by:
   a. Bearing weight on his heels and lateral borders of his feet twenty-five percent of the time when walking without shoes.
   b. Increasing shoulder stability so that he can use his arms to hang onto a moving piece of equipment for two minutes.
4. Improve self-help skills as demonstrated by:
   a. Feeding himself a soft food using a spoon, with minimal help.
   b. Drinking, with only slight dribbling, from a small glass that he holds.

After three months of Milestones participation, Carl began receiving weekly individual physical therapy at the Ayres Clinic. In addition, the physical therapist advised other Milestones staff members on ways to discourage maladaptive motor patterns and encourage adaptive responses during play on moving equipment, sitting on the floor, or moving about the play areas. The physical therapist gave the staff specific suggestions that combined neurodevelopmental treatment techniques with sensory integration treatment principles. For example, the physical therapist demonstrated how to manually provide tactile-proprioceptive input to his pelvic area while he was standing on a platform swing so that he reduced fixation of his leg and foot muscles, bore more weight on his heels, and improved his postural adjustments in response to the moving surface.

At Milestones, Carl was exposed to a variety of tactile media through free play, crafts, and center activities. He performed activities to develop his oral motor and feeding skills during the Pre-speech/Pre-feeding Center time and Snack Time. He had opportunities to improve his fine motor skills such as fingertip manipulation of objects (pegs and crayons) and drawing.

By five months of Milestones attendance, Carl was able to achieve all initial goals and objectives for his Milestones participation except for Goal 3, which was related to gross motor abilities. He did not achieve the objectives concerning weight bearing on his heels and shoulder stability. In the next month (when he was twenty-five months old), the staff administered the *EIDP*. The assessment results indicated Carl was demonstrating the following: language skills at nine to eleven months, feeding and gross motor skills at twelve to fifteen months, cognitive skills at twenty to twenty-three months, and social-emotional skills at twenty-four to twenty-seven months. Subsequent to this evaluation, Carl also began attending individual speech therapy once weekly at the Ayres Clinic.

Carl continued participating in Milestones until he was three years old. For his last six-month period of program attendance, the goals and objectives were as listed below.

Final Program Goals/Objectives
1. Improve cognitive and fine motor skills as demonstrated by:
   a. Copying a simple block design.
   b. Making several straight cuts with scissors.
2. Improve language and communication skills as demonstrated by:
   a. Using two or three words consistently during the program session.
   b. Imitating two simple words immediately.
3. Improve gross motor skills as demonstrated by:
   a. Bearing weight on the lateral borders of his feet twenty-five percent of the time when walking.
   b. Increasing shoulder stability for hanging from a moving piece of equipment.
   c. Increasing safety awareness to avoid walking into pieces of moving equipment.
4. Improve self-help skills as demonstrated by:
   a. Using the toilet and staying dry, one out of two program days each week.
   b. Pouring liquid from a small pitcher into a glass independently without spilling, three out of five times.

By three years of age, Carl had met all of his objectives except for Goal 3c (not walking into the path of moving equipment). Also, he still had a tendency to drool somewhat while drinking. He demonstrated improvement in his ability to follow directions and persist at tasks until he had completed them. Carl was an extremely happy and friendly child with a good attention span for fine motor tasks. He continued to experience difficulty modulating his movements and controlling his momentum. As a result, he often would run into things or fall down. When given verbal directions to slow down, walk on his heels, and look down before getting off of equipment, he was better able to control his movements. He was more willing to engage in tactile play than when he began the program. This suggested that his tactile defensiveness had lessened.

When retested with the *EIDP* at thirty-five months of age, Carl demonstrated age-appropriate skills except for significant delays in toilet training and self-feeding skills. However, due to his diagnosis of cerebral palsy and continuing risk of developmental delays, he met the criteria for acceptance into one of the preschool programs offered by his local school district. Prior to his discharge from Milestones, the program's staff and his case manager discussed Carl's strengths and remaining areas of concern, with his parents. The parents visited programs before selecting the one they believed would best meet Carl's needs. At age three, Carl transferred to that public school program. However, he continued to receive individual speech and physical therapy services at the Ayres Clinic.

Victor

Victor was a vivacious, dark-haired boy of Hispanic heritage. He lived with his adoptive parents who were Hispanic-American. When he began his three-times weekly attendance at the Milestones program, he was twenty-four months old. He had a diagnosis of developmental language and articulation disorder with borderline developmental delay. Victor had not been receiving any intervention services from the referring state agency.

Both parents participated actively in the program. Because the father had the more flexible work schedule, he was able to be present more frequently for the program sessions and monthly parent meetings. For the first few months that Victor attended the program, his father stayed with him throughout the program sessions. Once the father felt that Victor had made a successful adjustment to the program, the father no longer stayed for the whole session.

The parents initially expressed concern that Victor had delayed speech, was slow in learning things, became distracted easily, and had difficulty controlling his temper. They wished that he would learn how to play independently for a period of time, improve his concentration so that he could play with one toy for several minutes, and learn to share toys with other children.

Within the program setting Victor had difficulty transitioning between activities and leaving to go home. He would remain sitting for only a few minutes, even in a small group of two to three children. He used very few words and did not combine words. He had poor articulation and often relied on grunts or screams to communicate. Victor had difficulty waiting his turn and sharing with peers. He also had a poor awareness of safety. He would fall into other children and dive off of equipment. He required frequent verbal and physical cues to engage in gross motor activities safely.

On the basis of the parents' concerns, Victor's developmental history, and his actions in the program, the following goals and objectives were established for his first six months of program participation.

Initial Program Goals/Objectives

1. Improve organization of behavior as demonstrated by:
   a. Transitioning between each group without resisting, after one verbal prompt.
   b. Leaving for home at the session's end without becoming upset, eighty percent of the time.
   c. Remaining seated during Snack Time, with two verbal prompts during each session.
   d. Increasing his attention as evidenced by completing a structured task such as a simple puzzle, with only two prompts.
2. Increase sensory processing skills as demonstrated by:
   Using a protective extension response when attempting to dismount equipment, three out of five times.
3. Increase motor planning as demonstrated by:
   a. Dismounting equipment using his feet first, three out of five times.
   b. Manipulating a cause-and-effect toy successfully, three out of five times.
4. Improve speech and language as demonstrated by:
   a. Expressing his needs using one or two words such as "more juice."
   b. Pointing to one black-and-white picture on request.
5. Improve social skills as demonstrated by:
   Playing side-by-side once a week with another child without taking a toy from the child.

Victor's difficulties with focusing his attention and organizing his behavior appeared related to faulty processing and integration of visual, auditory, tactile-proprioceptive, and vestibular sensations. These apparent sensory integrative deficits probably contributed to his limited tolerance for riding on swings, tendency to propel his body roughly into people and surfaces, and inadequate safety precautions. Victor seemed particularly to benefit from the program's provision of enhanced sensations within the context of play activities. He enjoyed and sought out tactile-proprioceptive sensory experiences in particular. Often his length and degree of involvement in activities could be extended if a staff member interacted with him. The program's daily routine and transition signals seemed to help Victor prepare for the changes in sensations associated with different activities.

After four months of program attendance, Victor achieved all of his goals and objectives except for Goal 3a (dismounting equipment feet-first). He often dismounted equipment head-first.

When evaluated with the *EIDP* at twenty-nine months of age, he had a wide variance in developmental skills. He was performing cognitive skills from twelve to twenty-three months, self-care skills from sixteen to twenty-three months, language skills at twenty to twenty-three months, and perceptual/fine motor and social-emotional skills at twenty-four to twenty-seven months. He had some scattered skills up to thirty-five months.

The program director met with Victor's father to discuss the possibility that his son would benefit from both individual occupational and speech therapy. At the parents' request, a recommendation for individual speech therapy, only, was made to the referring agency. Following funding approval, Victor began attending weekly speech therapy at the Ayres Clinic.

Victor continued participation in Milestones until he was three years old. The following are the goals and objectives set for him to achieve during his last six months of program attendance.

Final Program Goals/Objectives
1. Improve organization of behavior as demonstrated by:
   a. Improving environmental awareness, such as not walking in front of a moving piece of equipment, three out of five times.
   b. Completing a routine task such as getting on a mat for Circle Time with only two verbal prompts, two out of three times a week.
   c. Leaving a favorite activity with moderate prompting from a staff member one time per week.
2. Improve ability to use sensory information effectively as demonstrated by:
   a. Remaining on a piece of moving equipment for two minutes during each program session.
   b. Maintaining his balance on an unstable piece of equipment for fifteen to thirty seconds, three out of five times.
3. Improve motor planning skills as demonstrated by:
   a. Dismounting equipment feet-first instead of "crashing" off equipment, seventy-five percent of the time during each session.
   b. Imitating unseen body movements immediately and exactly on three occasions.
4. Improve cognitive skills as demonstrated by:
   a. Matching two sets of objects by color on three occasions.
   b. Completing a three-piece puzzle with only verbal encouragement.
5. Improve his social skills as demonstrated by:
   Participating in turn-taking activities with staff or peers once during each session.
6. Improve his language and communication skills as demonstrated by:
   Saying his own name when asked, "What is your name?" twice per week.

By the end of his participation in Milestones, Victor was successfully able to achieve all of his final program goals and objectives except Goals 1a,

2b, and 3a, which were related to safety awareness, sensory processing, and motor planning. Although Victor had shown some improvement, he failed to exercise sufficient caution when crossing in the path of moving equipment and dismounting equipment. Although Victor would not consistently ride on a piece of moving equipment during each session, he did initiate riding on such equipment more frequently than before. Victor still had some difficulty in maintaining his balance on such equipment. Additionally, he had some trouble reproducing shapes by drawing and building with blocks. However, Victor was able to initiate play with toys and attend to activities for several minutes on some occasions. When extraneous distractions were reduced, he could concentrate better. He demonstrated concern and affection for peers and could share toys somewhat. He enjoyed domestic play and would engage in interactive play at times. Although he continued to have some articulation difficulties, Victor used language to express his wants, desires, and feelings. He usually was cooperative with the staff but still tended to become "disorganized" when he received multiple, intense stimulation from the environment or had to adapt to a change in the routine. If he was placed in a quiet environment away from activity and people at such times, he could calm down and reorganize his behavior.

The results of his developmental assessment when he was thirty-five months old indicated that Victor was demonstrating developmental skills at an age-appropriate level except for perceptual, fine motor, and language skills, which were at the twenty-eight- to thirty-one-month level. Because Victor's developmental scores were too high to qualify him for placement in a preschool program for children with special needs, the Milestones staff provided some information about possible community programs. The parents did additional investigation and selected a preschool program administered by the local YMCA. Victor began attending that program following his discharge from the Milestones program.

SUMMARY

As Melissa, Carl, and Victor participated in the Milestones program, each achieved gains in developmental skills that were greater than would be expected by maturation alone. Eventually they all interacted with objects, the environment, and people with greater focus, ease, pleasure, and complexity than before their program participation. In addition, the parents of these three children demonstrated increased understanding of their child's capabilities and needs, knowledge of ways to foster their child's development, and awareness of resources to assist them in meeting their child's needs. These case examples indicate the effectiveness of the Milestones program.

The efficacy of the Milestones program is related to the values and beliefs that guided its creation and management. Foremost is the premise that facilitating normal sensory integration processes is critical to the development of young children. Second is the emphasis on the partnership between the program staff and families that actively involves the families.

Third is the multidisciplinary composition of the staff and the program's attention to all domains that appear to lead to corresponding improvements in every area of development.

Another important aspect is the program's design and environment, which encourage interaction between the children and families and prepares the children for participation in community-based group programs. An additional factor is the aim of the staff to tailor the group program to best meet the needs of each individual child and family. All of these elements have combined to make Milestones a successful early intervention program that can serve as a model for programs elsewhere.

Program Parent Handbook

Parents and program staff may find that a handbook including information about the following topics is helpful.

I. Program description
    A. Staffing
        1. Professional disciplines
        2. Group size and staff/child ratio
    B. Entrance and exit criteria
    C. Session days and times
    D. Overall goals of program
    E. Type of activities/therapy equipment
    F. Example of weekly schedule
    G. Family involvement
        1. Session participation
        2. Monthly newsletter
        3. Parent meetings
II. Policies and procedures
    A. Transportation
        1. Times for drop-off and pick-up
        2. Written permission for individuals other than parents
    B. Absences/attendance
    C. Health issues
        1. Immunizations
        2. Allergies
        3. Medications
        4. Illness
        5. Ongoing conditions related to eating, physical limitations, and medical diagnoses
    D. Emergency situations
        1. Medical emergencies
        2. Seizures
        3. Natural disasters
    E. Toilet training/diapers
    F. Birthday celebrations

G. Discipline
H. Documentation
    1. Goals and objectives
    2. Assessments
    3. Reports

Child and Family Information Questionnaire

It may be helpful to have the following information about the child and family recorded on one or more written forms.

I. Basic Data
   A. Names, home and work addresses, home and work telephone numbers, Social Security numbers of child, parents, and/or legal guardian
   B. Child's birth date and gender
   C. Referral source
   D. Reason for referral
   E. Family's primary language/need for interpreter
   F. Alternative emergency contact person
   G. Names and phone numbers of individuals (other than parents) allowed to pick up child
   H. Medical insurance company, phone number, and policy number
II. Supplemental Information
   A. Medical/health information
       1. Existence of diagnosis
       2. Allergies
       3. Seizure history
       4. Medications
       5. Other medical/health conditions affecting child's activities
       6. Eating/drinking difficulties
       7. Physician name and address
       8. Immunizations
   B. Involvement in other intervention services
   C. Involvement in community-based programs

Family Perspective Questionnaire

Below are sample questions that could be included in a written questionnaire or asked verbally during a parent interview.

- What is a typical day like for your child?
- What would make the day easier for your child and family?
- What are some of your child's favorite activities?
- What do you see as your child's strengths?
- What are your major concerns about your child's development?
- What would you like your child to gain from the program?
- What would you like to learn from the program?
- Do you plan to attend the program regularly with your child?
- Would you be interested in and able to attend parent meetings held during program sessions once every four to six weeks?
- Do you have any other questions, concerns, or comments?

Weekly Schedule 2 Example

The following is an example of a weekly schedule of activities based on a set of monthly concepts. The equipment set up for the Sensory Motor Integration and Gross Motor/Language Center usually remains the same for the whole week. The activities for the other centers and time periods would be selected from the weekly list. Some of the activities would be repeated over the week (e.g., singing the concept-related songs) and others would not be repeated (e.g., painting yellow ducks). This sample weekly schedule would reinforce the concepts of *yellow, triangle,* and *up/down.*

9:30–10:00 a.m., **Exploratory Play**

Paint yellow ducks
Play in a pool of cornmeal
Build with yellow cardboard blocks

10:00–10:45 a.m., **Centers**

Sensory Motor Integration
Climb up triangular foam structure to ball pool
Walk up and down blue ramp
Ride in yellow chair swing
Ride on tire swing

Cognitive/Language
Say giraffe rhyme
Wear yellow hat
Match colored balls
Place triangle form in form board

Gross Motor/Language
Jump on yellow trampoline
Obstacle course:
  Crawl through red-and-yellow tunnel, climb up onto and jump
    down from yellow circular platform, and climb up and down
    large triangular structure.

Pre-speech/Pre-feeding
Blow yellow cotton balls with blowpipes
Name yellow foods
Quack while wearing yellow duck masks
Lick lemon yogurt off lips
Use toothbrushes with lemon drink
Find triangle shapes hidden in rice

10:45–11:00 a.m., **Movement to Music**

"Ring Around the Rosie"
Freeze Dance

11:00–11:15 a.m., **Snack Time**

Corn muffins and orange/pineapple juice
Triangular crackers and lemonade
Banana slices and apple juice

11:15–11:30 a.m., **Circle Time**

"Here We Are Together"
"Color Song"
"Five Little Ducks"
Two selections from song sheets
Sharing toys from home
"Good-bye Song"

Play Dough Recipe

2 cups white flour
1/2 cup table salt
4 teaspoons cream of tartar
2 cups water
2 tablespoons vegetable oil
A few drops of food coloring
Wax paper

Mix all ingredients except food coloring in a bowl. It will be runny. If multiple colors are desired, divide the dough and add a different color to each portion. Cook the dough (different colors separately) in a frying pan over medium heat. An electric frying pan set at 350 degrees works well for this. Stir over heat until the mixture sets and dries out (five to ten minutes). Remove the dough from the pan and place it on wax paper. Let it cool for ten minutes, then knead the dough a few times. Place the dough in an airtight container for storage.

Seizure Information Sheet

If the program population includes a child who experiences seizures periodically, the following information on a form completed by the parent would be helpful to the program staff.

    I. Seizure description
        A. Frequency
        B. Length
        C. Signs of seizure
        D. Possible triggers
   II. Responses to seizure occurrence
        A. Recommended steps for staff to take
        B. Calling 911
        C. Transportation to hospital
        D. Notification of physician or other person besides parents
  III. Insurance coverage

Early Intervention Developmental Profile Sample Page*

Perceptual/Fine Motor

Item Number	Developmental Levels and Items	Date	Date	Date	Date

12–15 months

Item Number	Developmental Levels and Items	Date	Date	Date	Date
22	Turns page of cardboard book				
23	Removes cover from small square box				
24	Places one or two pegs in pegboard				
25	Builds two-cube tower				
26	Scribbles spontaneously (no demonstration)				
27	Releases raisin into small bottle				

16–19 months

Item Number	Developmental Levels and Items	Date	Date	Date	Date
28	Places six pegs in pegboard without help				
29	Builds three-cube tower				
30	Places round form in form board (three forms presented)				
31	Imitates crayon stroke				

*Reprinted with permission from the University of Michigan Press S. J. Rogers, C. M. Donovan, D. B. D'Eugenio, S. L. Brown, E. W. Lynch, M. S. Moersch, and D. S. Schafer. 1981. Early Intervention Developmental Profile. In *Developmental programming for infants and young children,* revised ed., Vol. 2, edited by D. S. Schafer and M. S. Moersch.

20–23 months

32	Places six pegs in pegboard in 34 seconds				
33	Makes vertical and circular scribble after demonstration				
34	Completes three-piece form board				
35	Builds six-cube tower				
36	Holds crayon with fingers				
37	Attempts to fold paper imitatively				

24–27 months

38	Draws vertical and horizontal strokes imitatively				
39	Completes reversed form board				
40	Aligns two or more cubes for train, no smokestack				
41	Unscrews jar lid				
42	Scribbles with circular motion				

Resources

Books

Caregiver education guide for children with developmental disabilities.
S. Niemeyer. 1994. Aspen Reference Group. Aspen Publishers, Inc.,
200 Orchard Ridge Dr., Gaithersburgh, MD 20878. 800-638-8437.

*Combining neuro-developmental treatment and sensory integration
principles: An approach to pediatric therapy.* E. I. Blanche,
T. M. Botticelli, and M. K. Hallway. 1995. Communication/Therapy
Skill Builders, 555 Academic Court, San Antonio, TX 78204-2498.
800-228-0752.

*Developing integrated programs: A transdisciplinary approach for
early intervention.* M. C. Coling. 1991. Communication/Therapy
Skill Builders, 555 Academic Court, San Antonio, TX 78204-2498.
800-228-0752.

Developmental dyspraxia and adult-onset apraxia. A. J. Ayres. 1985.
Sensory Integration International, 1602 Cabrillo Ave., Torrance, CA
90501. 310-320-9986.

M.O.R.E.: Integrating the mouth. P. Oetter, E. Richter, and S. M. Frick.
1993. PDP Press, 14398 N. 59th St., Oak Park Heights, MN 55082.
612-439-8865.

More piggyback songs. J. Warren. 1984. Frank Schaffer Publications,
P.O. Box 2853, Torrance, CA 90509. 800-421-5565.

Movement is fun: A preschool movement program. S. B. Young. 1988.
Sensory Integration International, 1602 Cabrillo Ave., Torrance, CA
90501. 310-320-9986.

Occupational therapy for children (3rd ed). J. Case-Smith, A.S. Allen,
and P. N. Pratt, eds. 1996. Mosby-Year Book, Inc., 11830 Westline
Industrial Drive, St. Louis, MO 63146-9934. 800-426-4545.

Occupational therapy services for children and youth under the Individuals with Disabilities Education Act. E. Maruyama, G. Chandler, G. F. Clark, R. W. Dick, M. C. Lawlor, and L. L. Jackson. 1997. The American Occupational Therapy Association, Inc., AOTA Products, P.O. Box 31220, Bethesda, MD 20824-1220. 800-SAY-AOTA (members), 800-377-8555 (TDD), 301-652-2682 (non-members).

Pediatric occupational therapy and early intervention. J. Case-Smith. 1993. Andover Medical Publishers, P.O. Box 4500, Woburn, MA 01801. 800-366-2665.

Piggyback songs. J. Warren. 1983. Frank Schaffer Publications, P.O. Box 2853, Torrance, CA 90509. 800-421-5565.

Piggyback songs for infants and toddlers. J. Warren. 1985. Frank Schaffer Publications, P.O. Box 2853, Torrance, CA 90509. 800-421-5565.

Play in occupational therapy for children. L. D. Parham and L. S. Fazio. 1997. Mosby-Year Book, Inc., 11830 Westline Industrial Drive, St. Louis, MO 63146-9934. 800-426-4545.

Pre-feeding skills: A comprehensive resource for feeding development. S. E. Morris and M. D. Klein. 1987. Communication/Therapy Skill Builders, 555 Academic Court, San Antonio, TX 78204-2498. 800-228-0752.

Sensory integration: Theory and practice. A. G. Fisher, E. A. Murray, and A. C Bundy, eds. 1991. F. A. Davis Company, 1915 Arch St., Philadelphia, PA 19013. 800-523-4049.

Sensory integration and the child. A. J. Ayres. 1979. Western Psychological Services, 12031 Wilshire Blvd., Los Angeles, CA 90025-1251. 800-648-8857.

Sensory integration and learning disorders. A. J. Ayres. 1979. Western Psychological Services, 12031 Wilshire Blvd., Los Angeles, CA 90025-1251. 800-648-8857.

Cassette Tapes/Records

Individualization in movement and music. R. Hallum and H. B. Glass. Educational Activities, Inc., P.O. Box 392, Freeport, NY 11520. 800-645-3739.

More singable songs. Raffi. A & M Records.

Preschool aerobic fun. Kimbo Educational, P.O. Box 477, Long Branch, NJ 07740. 800-631-2187.

Singable songs for the very young. Raffi. A & M Records.

Sounds like fun. Discovery Toys, P.O. Box 5023, Livermore, CA 94551. 800-426-4777 (call for local distributor).

Catalogs

Abilitations by Sportime, One Sportime Way, Atlanta, GA 30340. 800-850-8602. (Equipment, manipulatives, and toys).

Achievement Products, P.O. Box 9033, Canton, OH 44711. 800-373-4699. (Equipment, manipulatives, and toys).

AOTA Products, The American Occupational Therapy Association, Inc., P.O. Box 31220, Bethesda, MD 20824-1220. 800-SAY-AOTA (members), 800-377-8555 (TDD), 301-652-2682 (non-members). (Books).

Childcraft, P.O. Box 1811, Peoria, IL 61656. 800-631-5657. (Equipment and toys).

Communication/Therapy Skill Builders, 555 Academic Court, San Antonio, TX 78204-2498. 800-228-0752. (Books, handouts, and videos).

Discovery Toys, P.O. Box 5023, Livermore, CA 94551. 800-426-4777 (call for local distributor). (Books, cassette tapes, and toys).

Equipment Shop, Inc., P.O. Box 33, Bedford, MA 01730. 800-525-7681. (Eating aids, equipment, and oral motor tools).

Flaghouse, 601 Route 46 West, Hasbrouck Heights, N.J. 07604. 800-793-7900. (Equipment).

Lakeshore Learning Material, 2695 E. Dominguez St., Carson, CA 90749. 800-421-5354. (Arts/crafts supplies, books, cognitive and language materials, equipment, furniture, and toys, including those made of tactile materials).

Lilly's Kids, Lillian Vernon Corp., 100 Lillian Vernon Dr., Virginia Beach, VA 23479-0002. 800-285-5555. (Manipulatives and toys).

One Step Ahead, 75 Albrecht Dr., Lake Bluff, IL 60044. 800-274-8440. (Toys, toy storage units, and trampolines).

PDP Products, 14398 N. 59th St., Oak Park Heights, MN 55082. 612-439-8865. (Books and equipment/supplies for oral motor and tactile activities).

Perfectly Safe, 4450 Belden Village St. N.W., Suite 406, Canton, OH 44718. 800-837-KIDS. (Chair with tray and safety supplies).

Play Fair Toys, P.O. Box 18210 Boulder, CO 80308. 800-824-7255. (Non-violent toys).

PRO-ED, 8700 Shoal Creek Blvd., Austin, TX 78757-6897. 800-897-3202. (Books, parent handouts, and photo cards).

Sammons Preston, P.O. Box 5071, Bolingbrook, IL 60440-5071. 800-323-5547. (Eating aids, equipment, manipulatives, and toys).

Southpaw Enterprises, Inc., P.O. Box 1047, Dayton, OH 45401-1047. 800-228-1698. (Equipment, manipulatives, and oral motor toys).

Therapro, 225 Arlington St., Framingham, MA 01702. 508-872-9494. (Books, equipment, supplies, and toys).

Toys To Grow On, 2695 E. Dominguez St., Carson, CA 90749. 800-542-8338. (Toys).

Handouts/Pamphlets

A parent's guide to understanding sensory integration. Sensory Integration International, 1602 Cabrillo Ave., Torrance, CA 90501. 310-320-9986.

"Caution: Children at work" poster. Sensory Integration International, 1602 Cabrillo Ave., Torrance, CA 90501. 310-320-9986.

Parent articles for early intervention. M. D. Klein, ed. 1990. Communication/Therapy Skill Builders, 555 Academic Court, San Antonio, TX 78204-2498. 800-228-0752.

Parent articles 1: Enhance parent involvement in language learning. M. Schrader, ed. 1988. Communication/Therapy Skill Builders, 555 Academic Court, San Antonio, TX 78204-2498. 800-228-0752.

Parent handout notepads. PRO-ED #1076. PRO-ED, 8700 Shoal Creek Blvd., Austin, TX 78757-6897. 800-897-3202.

Glossary

Accommodation   The process of adjusting one's thinking and actions to a new experience. Example: changing from using a gross grasp to using a fingertip grasp to pick up a crayon, and purposefully making marks with it. See *assimilation*.

Adaptive response   A purposeful and goal-directed behavior made in anticipation of or in response to an environmental challenge. Example: pushing off with one's feet to propel a swing.

Assimilation   The process of taking in new information and incorporating it into one's existing experience or pattern of activity. Example: picking up a large crayon with the whole hand, banging on a table with it, and noting that marks result.

Auditory   Related to the sense of hearing.

Balance reactions   See *equilibrium reactions*.

Bilateral motor coordination   Ability to move body parts harmoniously on both sides of the body simultaneously or alternately.

Body scheme or percept   Internal image of one's body, including overall size, location of body parts, relationship of body parts to one another, and possibilities of movement for each body part.

Cause and effect   Related to the recognition of what makes things occur and involvement of adults as causal agents. Example: a child patting an adult on the hand to signal the adult to wind up the jack-in-the-box toy again.

Cognition   Process of thinking, knowing, and problem solving.

Developmental domain   Category of behaviors that reflect a particular progression in development related to experience and maturity. Example: gross motor skills.

Discrimination   Recognition of and responsiveness to differences in stimuli. Example: selection of a circle shape, upon request, from a set of circles and squares.

Distal   At some distance from the trunk of the body.

Dyspraxia   Clumsiness in movement resulting from difficulties in conceiving, planning, and/or executing movements.

Environment   Surroundings, including the conditions and situations affecting the current behavior and ongoing development of a person.

Equilibrium reactions or responses   Automatic movement patterns of the whole body in order to maintain or re-establish the body's center of gravity over a base of support in response to movement of the body or surface.

Execution   The performance of a series of actions with the correct sequence, timing, and coordination. The phase of praxis that carries out the motor plan.

Expressive language   Communication of one's thoughts and feelings by the use of vocal sounds (e.g., spoken words), body movements (e.g., gestures or facial expressions), or written symbols (e.g., written words).

Extension   The action of straightening body part(s); straightened position.

Extensor   A muscle that straightens a body part.

Extremities   Arms (upper) and legs (lower).

Family-centered care   The provision of services to a child with special needs and to that child's family in a way that the family's strengths and uniqueness are recognized and its decision-making role encouraged.

Feedback   Sensory information from the muscles, joints, skin, and gravity/motion detectors during movement and sensory information from the environment that changes as a consequence of the action. This sensory information is used by the central nervous system to determine whether a correction in the response is needed. Example: tucking one's head lower after the head has grazed the top of a tire tunnel.

Feedforward   Internal feedback by which a motor command is compared to a sensory reference of correctness before the action occurs. Example: moving hands into position to catch a bounced ball.

Fine motor   Related to small movements of body part(s).

Flexion   The action of bending body part(s); bent position.

Flexor   A muscle that bends a body part.

Form constancy   Recognition of the consistency in the general pattern and structure of a type of visual stimuli, in spite of differences related to size, color, angle of vision, or other details. Example: knowing that a button, plate, and wheel are circles.

Gross motor   Related to large movements of body part(s).

Gross motor coordination   Smooth, well-timed movements of body part(s) in large patterns. Example: climbing or jumping.

Gustatory   Related to sense of taste.

Ideation   The process of conceiving ideas about what actions to take with objects and people in the environment. It is the phase of praxis involving anticipation of a desired result.

Interactive play   Play that involves some eye contact and turn-taking between two children or a child and an adult. The amount and complexity of interaction increases with the child's progressive development.

Kinesthesia   See *proprioception*.

Manipulation   Skillful handling of an object by hand(s).

Means-end   Related to recognition of how to produce a desired result, and involvement of problem solving with objects. Example: pulling a string to make a toy move.

Modulation   The process of appropriately balancing the influence of incoming sensory stimulation by facilitating certain sensory input to enhance the response and inhibiting or filtering certain sensory input to prevent distraction or excessive arousal. Examples: (1) ignoring the feel of sand on one's foot when searching with one's hand for a toy hidden in the sand and (2) not becoming distracted by other objects in a picture when asked to find one particular item in that picture.

Motor   Related to movement of the body.

Motor planning   The process of figuring out and organizing a series of actions necessary to complete an unfamiliar activity. This phase of praxis involves the ability to imagine what could result from various actions.

Muscle tone   The amount of tension in a muscle at rest. Abnormal muscle tone includes a greater than normal resistance to stretch or, conversely, less resistance than normal.

Object permanence   The ability to maintain a visual representation of an object when it no longer is visible, and being able to think of where it might be hidden.

Occupation   A culturally defined, purposeful activity that requires a period of time to complete. Daily occupations include those activities that are performed once or more daily, such as eating and dressing.

Oculomotor   Related to eye movements.

Olfactory   Related to the sense of smell.

Oral motor   Related to movements of the lips, cheeks, tongue, and jaw.

Organization of behavior   The ability to focus and sustain one's attention, initiate and complete activities, follow a routine, and adapt to changing situations while interacting with objects and people in one's environment.

Perception   The process by which the central nervous system organizes, interrelates, and assigns meaning to sensory information. It involves relating new sensory input to memories of previous experiences. Example: recognizing that a blue button is circular just as is the black wheel on a toy car.

Postural control   The process of "regulating the body's position in space for the dual purposes of stability and orientation" (Shumway-Cook and Woollacott 1995, 459).

Postural integration   The ability to respond with postural reactions (see next) to impending loss of balance, and make subtle, anticipatory adjustments of a body part's position relative to the position of another body part, during movement (postural background movements).

Postural reactions   Automatic responses of body parts to movement that align head and trunk (righting reactions), sustain or regain balance (equilibrium reactions), and protect against a fall (protective reactions).

Praxis   The process of thinking about, planning, and carrying out skilled, adaptive interactions with people and objects. It involves the organized use of time and space. Example: building a pretend house using blocks.

Prone   Position of lying on one's abdomen; position of one's hand with the palm facing down.

Proprioception   Related to the sense of movement and position of the body parts. Awareness originating from one's physical actions and stimulating sensors in muscles, joints, and skin; and comparison of those actions with a centrally generated motor command.

Proximal   At a point that is close to the trunk of the body.

Quadruped   Body position in which the four extremities are bearing weight on a surface.

Receptive language   Recognition and understanding of thoughts and feelings conveyed by vocal sounds (e.g., spoken words), body movements (e.g., gestures or facial expressions), or written symbols (e.g., written words).

Release   Letting go of something that had been grasped.

Righting reactions   Movements that allow one to assume or resume a particular orientation of the body or body parts in relation to the environment (Shumway-Cook and Woollacott 1995, 460).

Self-care skills   The abilities related to the independent performance of eating, drinking, dressing, grooming, and personal hygiene tasks.

Sensory input   Information about one's body and the external environment arising from one or more of the sensory systems.

Sensory integration   (1) Theory developed by Dr. A. Jean Ayres to explain the relationships between neurological processes, sensory motor behavior, and academic and social-emotional functioning; (2) The process of the nervous system (particularly at the brain-stem level) that combines, associates, interprets, and organizes sensory information from one's body and the environment. Successful integration of sensory information enables one to engage in effective environmental and social interactions.

Sensory integrative dysfunction   A developmental disorder resulting from difficulties in the central integration of sensory input from the tactile, proprioceptive, and vestibular sensory systems. These difficulties are not caused by peripheral or cortical central nervous system dysfunction. This disorder is characterized by mild to moderate inadequacies in behavior and learning.

Sensory Motor Integration Center   An area in which a small group of children engages in activities that provide motion, tactile, and proprioceptive sensory experiences, and involve motor planning. The children are challenged by the environment, and the center leaders direct the actions of their bodies to achieve a goal such as maintaining balance on a moving swing or sliding into a pool of balls. The center leaders observe each child's responses and make changes in the environment or activity so that each child has the appropriate sensory input and challenge.

Sensory processing   The process by which the nervous system takes in, recognizes, and assigns significance to information arising from one of the various sensory systems. The latter step involves inhibiting or enhancing perception of this information. Finally, the process organizes sensory information for use in selecting and planning adaptive behavior.

Sensory registration   The process by which the central nervous system notes that certain sensory input is being received. A well-functioning central nervous system will notice the introduction of new sensory input or changes in the existing sensory input.

Somatosensory   Related to tactile and proprioceptive sensory input.

Stereognosis   The process of identifying an object in one's hand by relying on tactile and proprioceptive input alone, without using visual information.

Stimulation   Sensory input that elicits a response.

Supine   The position of lying on one's back; position of one's hand with the palm facing up.

Tactile   Related to the sense of touch.

Tactile defensiveness   The tendency to react negatively and emotionally (e.g., withdrawing from or striking at the source of the stimulus, or being excessively excited and active) to touch sensations that most people consider to be non-offensive. Examples: refusing to walk barefoot on the grass or hitting someone after being accidentally bumped.

Tactile tolerance   The ability to experience and seek out various types of touch sensations without becoming unusually upset, distracted, or excited.

Turn-taking   The process of performing an action and then waiting while another person performs an action. It is involved in many social interactions including conversation and play with others.

Ulnar-to-radial sequence   Progression from the little finger side of the hand to the thumb side of the hand.

Verbalization   The production of sound having specific meaning (i.e., word or word approximation).

Vestibular   Related to the sense of head position and movement of the body through space.

Visual accommodation   The adjustment process of the lens of the eyes to permit focusing on objects at different distances.

Visual pursuit   The process of the eyes tracking a moving target (object or person of interest).

Vocalization   The production of sound that may or may not have specific, associated meaning. Examples of the latter type of vocalization: a baby's babbling or a child's whoop.

Weight bearing   The act of supporting a portion or all of one's body weight on one or more parts of the body, such as the feet.

Weight shifting   Changing the distribution of body weight borne by one or more parts of the body to another part or parts. Example: when walking up steps, transferring one's body weight from the right leg and foot to the left leg and foot.

References

Als, H. 1986. A syntactive model of neonatal behavioral organization: Framework for the assessment of neurobehavioral development in the premature infant and for support in infants and parents in the neonatal intensive care environment. *Physical and Occupational Therapy in Pediatrics* 6 (3/4, fall/winter): The high-risk neonate developmental therapy perspective.

Als, H., B. Lester, and T. B. Brazelton. 1979. Dynamics of the behavioral organization of the premature infant: A theoretical perspective. In *Infants Born at Risk,* ed. T. Field, A. Millaresco, S. Goldberg, and H. Shuman, 173–92. New York: SP Medical and Scientific Books.

Ayres, A. J. 1972. *Sensory integration and learning disorders.* Los Angeles: Western Psychological Services.

_____. 1979. *Sensory integration and the child.* Los Angeles: Western Psychological Services.

_____. 1984. Personal communication.

_____. 1985. *Developmental dyspraxia and adult onset apraxia.* Torrance, CA: Sensory Integration International.

_____. 1989. *Sensory integration and praxis test—SIPT manual.* Los Angeles: Western Psychological Services.

Blanche, E. I. *The organization of one's behavior in space and time.* (Unpublished manuscript).

_____. 1988. Intervention for motor control and movement organization disorders. In *Pediatric occupational therapy and early intervention,* 2d ed., ed. J. Case-Smith, 255–76. Woburn, MA.: Butterworth-Heineman.

Blanche, E. I., and J. P. Burke. 1991. Combining neurodevelopmental and sensory integration approaches in the treatment of the neurologically impaired child. Parts 1 and 2. *Sensory Integration Quarterly* 19: (1) 1–5, (2) 1–6.

Blanche, E. I., T. M. Botticelli, and M. K. Hallway. 1995. *Combining neuro-developmental treatment and sensory integration principles: An approach to pediatric therapy.* San Antonio: Therapy Skill Builders.

Bloom, L., and M. Lakey. 1978. *Language development and language disorders.* New York: John Wiley & Sons.

Bly, L. 1983. *The components of normal movement during the first year of life and abnormal motor development.* Monograph. Chicago: Neuro-Developmental Treatment Association, Inc.

———. 1994. *Motor skills acquisition in the first year: An illustrated guide to normal development.* San Antonio: Therapy Skill Builders.

Bobath, B. 1963. Treatment principles and planning in cerebral palsy. *Physiotherapy* 49:122–24.

———. 1967. The very early treatment of cerebral palsy. *Developmental Medicine and Child Neurology* 9:373–90.

Bobath, K., and B. Bobath. 1964. The facilitation of normal postural reactions and movements in the treatment of cerebral palsy. *Physiotherapy* 50:246–62.

Brazelton, T. B. 1973. Neonatal behavioral assessment scale. *Clinics in Developmental Medicine No. 50.*

Bronfenbrenner, U. 1979. *The ecology of human development: Experiments by nature and design.* Cambridge, MA: Harvard University.

Bruner, J. 1986. *Acts of meaning.* Cambridge, MA: Harvard University.

Busch-Rossnagel, N. 1997. Mastery motivation in toddlers. *Infants and Young Children* 9(4): 1–11.

Busey, T., and G. Loftus. 1994. Sensory and cognitive components of visual information acquisition. *Psychological Review* 101(3):446–69.

Bzoch, K. R., and R. League. 1991. *Receptive-expressive emergent language test: A method for accessing the language skills of infants.* 2d ed. Austin, TX: PRO-ED, Inc.

Cabanac, M. 1988. Pleasure (sensory). *Sensory systems II: Senses other than vision. Readings from the encyclopedia of neuroscience,* ed. J. Wolfe, 97–98. Boston: Birkhauser.

Case-Smith, J. 1997. Pediatric assessment. *OT Practice* 2(4):24–39.

Cermak, S. 1996. A. Jean Ayres Lectureship Award Presentation: The effect of deprivation on processing, play, and praxis. Presentation at the *1996 Symposium—Broadening the perspectives: Sensory processing aspects of learning and behavior.* June 1–2, 1996, San Diego, CA.

Cermak, S., and L. Daunhauer. 1997. Sensory processing in the postinstitutionalized child. *American Journal of Occupational Therapy,* 51(7):500–7.

Clakins, S. 1994. Origins and outcomes of individual differences in emotion regulation. *Monographs of the Society for Research in Child Development* 59:53–72.

Clark, F., and E. A. Larson. 1993. Developing an academic discipline: The science of occupation. In *Willard and Spackman's occupational therapy* (8th ed.), ed. H. L. Hopkins and H. D. Smith, 44–57. Philadelphia: J. B. Lippincott Company.

Clark, F., Z. Mailloux, and D. Parham. 1985. Sensory integration and children with learning disabilities. *Occupational therapy for children,* ed. P. N. Pratt and A. S. Allen, 305–405. St. Louis: Mosby.

Clark, F. A., D. Parham, M. E. Carlson, G. Frank, J. Jackson, D. Pierce, R. J. Wolfe, and R. Zemke. 1991. Occupational science: Academic innovation in the service of occupation therapy's future. *American Journal of Occupational Therapy* 45(4):300–12.

Colangelo, C., A. Bergen, and L. Gottlieb. 1976. *A normal baby: The sensory motor processes of the first year.* Valhalla, NY.: Blythdale Children's Hospital.

Cole, M. & S. Cole. 1989. *The development of children.* New York: Scientific American Books.

Cole, P., M. Michel, and L. Teti. 1994. The development of emotion regulation and dysregulation: A clinical perspective. *Monographs of the Society for Research in Child Development* 59(2–3):73–100.

Coley, I. L. 1978. *Pediatric assessment of self-care activities.* St. Louis: Mosby.

Connor, F., G. Williamson, and J. Siepp. 1978. *Program guide for infants and toddlers.* New York: Teachers College Press.

DeGangi, G. 1990. Perspective on the integration of neurodevelopmental treatment and sensory integrative therapy, Parts 1–3. *Neurodevelopmental Treatment Association Newsletter* (January):1, 4; (March):1, 6; (May):1, 5.

D'Eugenio, D. 1986. Infant play: A reflection of cognitive and motor development. In *Play: A skill for life*. Rockville, MD: The American Occupational Therapy Association, Inc.

DeMaio-Feldman, D. 1994. Somatosensory processing abilities of very low-birth weight infants at school age. *American Journal of Occupational Therapy* 48(7):639–45.

DesRosiers, F., and N. Busch-Rossnagel. 1997. Self-concept in toddlers. *Infants and Young Children* 10(1):15–26.

Diamond, M., R. Johnson, A. Protti, C. Ott, and L. Kajisa. 1985. Plasticity in the 904-day-old male rat cerebral cortex. *Experimental Neurology*. 87:309–17.

Dunst, C., C. Trivette, and A. Deal. 1989. A family systems assessment and intervention model. In *Family-centered care: An early intervention resource manual,* ed. B. E. Hanft, 2–66. Rockville, MD: The American Occupational Therapy Association, Inc.

Erhardt, R. 1986. *Erhardt developmental vision assessment.* Fargo, ND: R. Erhardt.

Exner, C. 1989. Development of hand functions. In *Occupational therapy for children.* 2d. ed. Edited by P. N. Pratt and A. S. Allen. St. Louis: Mosby.

Fagard, J. 1990. The development of bimanual coordination. In *Development of eye-hand coordination across the life span*, ed. C. Bard, M. Fleury, and L. Hay. Columbia: University of South Carolina Press.

Farber, S. 1982. *Neurorehabilitation—A multisensory approach.* Philadelphia: W. B. Saunders.

Fenson, L. 1985. The developmental progression of exploration and play. In *Play interactions: The role of toys and parental involvement in children's development,* ed. C. Caldwell Brown and A. Gottfried. Pediatric Round Table 11. Johnson & Johnson Baby Products Co.

Field, T. 1990. *Infancy.* Cambridge, MA: Harvard University Press.

Fiorentino, M. 1963. *Reflex testing methods for evaluating CNS development.* Springfield, IL: Charles Thomas Publisher.

Fisher, A. G. 1991. Vestibular-proprioceptive processing and bilateral integration and sequencing deficits. In *Sensory integration: Theory and practice,* ed. A. G. Fisher, E. A. Murray, and A. C. Bundy. Philadelphia: F. A. Davis Company.

Fisher, A. G., and E. A. Murray. 1991. Introduction to sensory integration theory. In *Sensory integration: Theory and practice,* ed. A. G. Fisher, E. A. Murray, and A. C. Bundy, 3–26. Philadelphia: F. A. Davis Company.

Florey, L. 1971. An approach to play and play development. *American Journal of Occupational Therapy* 25 (6):275–80.

Gesell, A., and F. Igi. 1949. *Child development: An introduction to the study of human growth.* New York: Harper.

Gessell, A., and C. S. Amatruda. 1974. *Developmental diagnosis.* Hagerstown, MD: Harper & Row.

Gilfoyle, E., A. Grady, and J. Moore. 1981. *Children adapt.* Thorofare, NJ: Charles Slack.

Ginsburg, H., and S. Opper. 1969. *Piaget's theory of intellectual development: An introduction.* Englewood Cliffs, NJ: Prentice-Hall.

Gisel, E. G. 1991. Effect of food texture on the development of chewing of children between six months and two years of age. *Developmental Medicine and Child Neurology* 33:69–79.

Gottlieb, G. 1983. The psychobiological approach to developmental issues. In *Handbook of child psychology,* 4th ed. Edited by P. Mussen. New York: John Wiley & Sons.

Grady, A. 1989. Foreword. In *Family-centered care: An early intervention resource manual,* ed. B. E. Hanft, *vii.* Rockville, MD: The American Occupational Therapy Association, Inc.

Graziadei, P. 1990. Olfactory development. In *Development of sensory systems in mammals,* ed. J. Colema, 519–51. New York: John Wiley & Sons.

Greenspan, S., and N. Greenspan. 1985. *First feelings: Milestones in the emotional development of your baby and child.* New York: Viking.

Gruber, H., and J. Voneche, eds. 1977. *The essential Piaget.* New York: Basic Books.

Haith, M. 1993. Preparing for the 21st century: Some goals and challenges for studies of infant sensory and perceptual development. *Developmental Review* 13:354–71.

Hanft, B. 1989. Providing family-centered occupational therapy services. *Sensory Integration Special Interest Section Newsletter* 12 (2):1–3.

Hatten, J. T., and P. Hatten. 1981. *Natural language.* San Antonio: Communication Skill Builders.

Heriza, C. 1991. Implications of a dynamical systems approach to understanding infant kicking behavior. *Physical Therapy* 71(3):54/ 222–67/235.

Kaplan, E. 1977. Praxis: Development. In *International Encyclopedia of Psychiatry, Psychology, Psychoanalysis, & Neurology.* Vol. 9, ed. B. Wolman. New York: Van Nostrand Reinhold Company.

Karniol, R. 1989. The role of manual manipulative stages in the infant's acquisition of perceived control over objects. *Developmental Review* 9:205–33.

Knobloch, H., and B. Pasamanick, eds. 1974. *Gesell and Amatruda's developmental diagnosis.* Hagerstown, MD: Harper and Row.

Kopp, C. 1982. Antecedents of self-regulation: A developmental perspective. *Developmental Psychology* 18 (2):199–214.

Lockman, J., and E. Thelen. 1993. Developmental biodynamics: Brain, body, behavior connections. *Child Development* 64:953–59.

Mack, W., J. Lindquist, and L. D. Parham. 1982. A synthesis of occupational behavior and sensory integration concepts in theory and practice: Parts 1 and 2. *American Journal of Occupational Therapy* 36:365–74, 433–37.

MacKay, D. 1985. A theory of the representation, organization and timing of action with implications for sequencing disorders. In *Neuropsychological studies of apraxia and related disorders,* ed. E. A. Roy. New York: Elsevier Science Publisher.

Majnemer, A., A. Brownstein, R. Kadanoff, and M. Y. Shevell. 1992. A comparision of neurobehavioral performance of healthy term and low-risk preterm infants at term. *Developmental Medicine and Child Neurology* 34:417–24.

Martin, B., Jr. 1992. *Brown bear, brown bear, what do you see?* New York: Henry Holt & Co.

McEwan, M., R. E. Dihoff, and G. M. Brosvic. 1991. Early infant crawling experience is reflected in later motor skill development. *Perceptual and Motor Skills* 73:75–79.

Miller, N. 1986. *Dyspraxia and its management.* Rockville, MD: Aspen.

Miller, R. 1988. What is theory and why does it matter? In *Six perspectives on theory for the practice of occupational therapy,* ed. B. Miller, K. Sieg, F. Ludgwig, S. Shortridge, and J. Van Deusen, 1–16. Rockville, MD: Aspen.

Mistretta, C. 1990. Taste development. In *Development of sensory systems in mammals*, ed. J. Colema, 519–51. New York: John Wiley & Sons.

Montagu, A. 1978. *Touching: The human significance of the skin.* New York: Harper & Row.

Morris, D. 1991. *Babywatching*. New York: Crown Publishers.

Mosey, A. 1989. The proper focus of scientific inquiry in occupational therapy: Frames of reference. *The Occupational Therapy Journal of Research* 9:195–201.

Neisworth, J. T., S. J. Bagnato, and J. Salvia. 1995. Neurobehavioral markers for early regulatory disorders. *Infants and Young Children* 8(1):8.

Parham, D. 1987. Toward professionalism: The reflective therapist. *American Journal of Occupational Therapy* 41:555–61.

Parham, L. D., and Z. Mailloux. 1996. Sensory integration. In *Occupational therapy for children* (3rd ed.), edited by A. S. Allen and P. N. Pratt, 307–52. St. Louis: Mosby.

Parham, L. D., and L. A. Primeau. 1997. Play and occupational therapy. In *Play in occupational therapy for children*, ed. L. D. Parham and L. S. Fazio, 2–21. St. Louis: Mosby.

Phillips, J. 1969. *The origins of intellect: Piaget's theory.* San Francisco: W. H. Freeman.

Piaget, J. 1952. *The origins of intelligence in children.* New York: International Universities Press, Inc.

Piaget, J., and B. Inhelder. 1969. *The psychology of the child.* New York: Basic Books, Inc.

Plomin, R. 1990. *Nature and nurture: An introduction to human behavioral genetics.* Pacific Grove, CA: Brooks/Cole Publishing Co.

Pulaski, M. 1980. *Understanding Piaget—An introduction to children's cognitive development,* 8–15. New York: Harper & Row.

Reilly, M., ed. 1974. *Play as exploratory learning.* Beverly Hills, CA: Sage Publications, Inc.

Robinson, A. 1977. Play: The arena for acquisition of rules for competent behavior. *American Journal of Occupational Therapy* 31:248–53.

Rock, I. 1975. *Introduction to perception.* New York: Macmillan.

Rogers, S. J., and D. B. D'Eugenio. 1981. Assessment and application. In *Developmental programming for infants and young children,* revised ed., Vol. 1, ed. D. S. Schafer and M. S. Moersch. Ann Arbor: The University of Michigan Press.

Rogers, S. J., C. M. Donovan, D. B. D'Eugenio, S. L. Brown, E. W. Lynch, M. S. Moersch, and D. S. Schafer. 1981. Early Intervention Developmental Profile. In *Developmental programming for infants and young children,* revised ed., Vol. 2, ed. D. S. Schafer and M. S. Moersch. Ann Arbor: The University of Michigan Press.

Sameroff, A. 1975. Transactional models in early social relations. *Human Development* 18:65–79.

Shaffer, D. 1988. *Social and personality development,* 2d. ed. Pacific Grove, CA: Brooks/Cole Publishing Co.

Short-DeGraff, M. 1988. *Human development for occupational and physical therapists.* Baltimore: Williams and Wilkins.

Shumway-Cook, A. and F. B. Horak. 1986. Assessing the influence of sensory interaction on balance: Suggestion from the field. *The Journal of American Physical Therapy Association.* 66(10):October.

Shumway-Cook, A., and M. Woollacott. 1995. *Motor control: Theory and application*, 459–60. Baltimore: Williams & Wilkins.

Vincent, L. J. 1989. What we have learned from families. *Family-centered care: An early intervention resource manual,* ed. B. E. Hanft, 4:7–8. Rockville, MD: The American Occupational Therapy Association, Inc.

White, B. 1975. *The first three years of life.* Englewood, NJ: Prentice-Hall.

Yerxa, E. J., F. Clark, G. Frank, J. Jackson, D. Parham, D. Pierce, C. Stein, and R. Zemke. 1990. An introduction to occupational science, A foundation for occupational therapy in the 21st century. *Occupational Therapy in Health Care* 6:1–17.

Young, P. T. 1959. The role of affective process in learning and motivation. *Psychology Review* 66:104–25.